*Dwight D. Eisenhower and
the Federal Highway Act*

LANDMARK PRESIDENTIAL DECISIONS

Series Editor
Michael Nelson

Advisory Board
Meena Bose
Brendan J. Doherty
Richard J. Ellis
Lori Cox Han
James Oakes
Barbara A. Perry
Andrew Rudalevige

Dwight D. Eisenhower and the Federal Highway Act

Charles U. Zug

University Press of Kansas

© 2024 by the University Press of Kansas
All rights reserved

Published by the University Press of Kansas (Lawrence, Kansas 66045), which was organized by the Kansas Board of Regents and is operated and funded by Emporia State University, Fort Hays State University, Kansas State University, Pittsburg State University, the University of Kansas, and Wichita State University.

Library of Congress Cataloging-in-Publication Data

Names: Zug, Charles U., author.
Title: Dwight D. Eisenhower and the Federal Highway Act / Charles U. Zug.
Description: Lawrence, Kansas : University Press of Kansas, 2024. | Series: Landmark presidential decisions | Includes bibliographical references and index.
Identifiers: LCCN 2023008557 (print) | LCCN 2023008558 (ebook)
  ISBN 9780700636006 (cloth)
  ISBN 9780700635993 (paperback)
  ISBN 9780700636013 (ebook)
Subjects: LCSH: United States.—Federal-Aid Highway Act of 1956—History. | Express highways—Law and legislation—United States—History—20th century. | Federal aid to transportation—United States—History—20th century. | United States—Politics and government—1953–1961. | Eisenhower, Dwight D. (Dwight David), 1890–1969—Influence.
Classification: LCC KF5530.A3281956 Z84 2024 (print) | LCC KF5530.A3281956 (ebook) | DDC 344.7304/7—dc23/eng/20230802
LC record available at https://lccn.loc.gov/2023008557.
LC ebook record available at https://lccn.loc.gov/2023008558.

British Library Cataloguing-in-Publication Data is available.

Printed in the United States of America

10 9 8 7 6 5 4 3 2 1

The paper used in this publication is acid free and meets the minimum requirements of the American National Standard for Permanence of Paper for Printed Library Materials Z39.48-1992.

For Mimi Zug

The political man is constantly forced to have very long conversations with very dull people on very dull subjects. Ninety-nine percent, if not more, of politics is administration. And as for the exciting part, the decision-making, it is inseparable from long periods of mere waiting—of an action which consists in the suspension of doing as well as of thinking.

Leo Strauss

CONTENTS

Foreword by Andrew Rudalevige   ix

Acknowledgments   xiii

Introduction: Presidential Decisions   1

Chapter 1. Background and Context, 1787–1952   11

Chapter 2. Presidential Initiative: Eisenhower's Initial Forays into Highway Expansion, 1952–1954   21

Chapter 3. The Clay Committee and the Development of Eisenhower's Highway Program, 1954–1955   39

Chapter 4. Congress Resurgent: The Defeat of the Eisenhower Highway Bill in 1955   63

Chapter 5. The Final Push and Congressional Victory   105

Conclusion   123

Notes   129

Bibliographic Essay   145

Index   149

About the Author   155

FOREWORD

Everyone knows that President Eisenhower built the highways. After all, every driver road-tripping their way across the United States—on I-95 from Portland, Maine, say, or I-5 out of Portland, Oregon—keeps seeing five-starred blue signs telling drivers they are on the "Eisenhower Interstate System," but more formally, federal law has decreed since 1990, the "Dwight D. Eisenhower National System of Interstate and Defense Highways." If those drivers pull over at a rest stop (perhaps on I-70 near Belmont, Ohio), they can park next to one of the large historical markers that portray their journey as part of Eisenhower's very genetic code, proclaiming him "father of the Interstate Highway System."

In this installment of the Landmark Presidential Decisions series, though, Charles U. Zug administers a paternity test to the 1956 Federal-Aid Highway Act. And he finds that, at best, Ike was a deadbeat dad.

In what follows, Zug carefully reconstructs the backstory of the famous law, starting with a long history of federal support for internal improvements in the United States. The need for a network of highways became clear in the automotive age, and a predecessor statute in 1938 provided a partial blueprint for what is now more than 45,000 miles of roads linking sea to shining sea.

Zug shows that Eisenhower's desire to significantly expand the highway system ran up against his strong sentiments against deficit spending. Zug quotes journalist Theodore White: "The politics of American highways has always been dominated by one overwhelming truth: everyone loves roads, but no one wants to pay for them." To square that circle, an advisory committee appointed by Eisenhower and led by his former US Army colleague Lucius Clay (the so-called Clay Committee) invented a financing mechanism that claimed to issue federal bonds for highway construction without those bonds counting against the national debt. It was a fiscal fiction that Eisenhower and his administration committed to, but one that undermined the plan's chance of ever becoming law.

The centralized process by which the committee drafted its report, eschewing congressional and federal agency involvement in its formulation, shows why Eisenhower's reputation as an adherent to "cabinet government" is far too simplistic. It shows, too, how the steps presidents take to control the executive branch, in this case to obtain the substantive legislation they want, can hurt that legislation's prospects at the other end of Pennsylvania Avenue. Here, Eisenhower hoped to dictate his plan to Congress. Lucius Clay was a direct descendant of Senator Henry Clay, but in contrast to his forebear, he quickly became known as "the Great Un-Compromiser." Congress, though, had plans of its own. Eisenhower staffer Jim Hagerty mournfully noted in his minutes of a February 1955 meeting between the president and legislative leadership that "the only good" resulting from the encounter "was this doodle which the President did while the meeting was going on."

As a result, Eisenhower's plan was soundly rejected on the Senate floor in 1955. Only later that year did the administration recalculate and recalibrate, scrapping the Clay Committee's financing plan and accepting increased user taxes; to this mix Secretary of the Treasury George Humphrey added the Highway Trust Fund as a way to keep those taxes from being siphoned into nonhighway spending. The subsequent bill, largely based on legislation proposed by Senator Albert Gore Sr. and Representative George Fallon, passed easily in 1956. Zug concludes, "It was congressional Democrats who salvaged interstate highway expansion after Eisenhower and his administration so clearly mismanaged it."

The story that follows, then, is a telling tale about presidents and the legislative process. It suggests the need for presidential flexibility and foresight—and for astute management both of policy formulation and its gauntlet to enactment. And it lays the groundwork, so to speak, for crucial aspects of US political development that would follow. The Interstate Highway System has helped knit together the vast geography of the postwar United States. Eisenhower said in 1955, "The united forces of our communication and transportation systems are dynamic elements in the very name we bear—United States." But those highways also led to the destruction of vibrant urban neighborhoods and the suburban sprawl that (as another astute observer put it) "paved paradise." Either way, the shape and scale of the decisions made nearly seventy years ago—by Dwight Eisenhower and many others—are undeniably important. Landmark, one might say.

Andrew Rudalevige
Bowdoin College

ACKNOWLEDGMENTS

Revised portions of this book appeared in *Presidential Studies Quarterly* 53, no. 1 (2023): 120–136. Permission to incorporate is gratefully acknowledged.

I would like to thank David Congdon and Michael Nelson for skillfully steering this project through the publication process. Michael Genovese and Dan Ponder provided extensive feedback on the manuscript, for which I am grateful. I also appreciate the efforts of Ariel Turley, Linda Smith, and everyone at the Dwight D. Eisenhower Library in Abilene, Kansas, who helped me access the archives during the COVID-19 pandemic. My former colleagues at the University of Colorado, Colorado Springs were an encouraging presence as I completed this project. I am particularly grateful to Joshua Dunn and the Center for the Study of Government and the Individual for financial and professional support.

For many of the historical and archival components of this project, I am indebted to a small but dedicated group of scholars whose work on US highways has proved indispensable. Tom Lewis was a helpful interlocutor and pointed me in the right direction when I began making my way through the Eisenhower Archives. Department of Transportation historian Richard Weingroff has written numerous essays on the history of the Interstate Highway System, and generously provided me with documents I was unable to locate on my own. My greatest debt of gratitude is to Jeff Davis at the Eno Center. In addition to dozens of archival documents, Jeff generously shared his wealth of knowledge about federal highways and President Eisenhower in the course of countless email conversations. I hope my book helps these scholars as much as their work has benefited mine.

In the course of two mid-pandemic, cross-country trips during the summers of 2020 and 2021, my wife, Mimi, and I gained a fuller appreciation of the Dwight D. Eisenhower Interstate Highway System than I suspect either of us ever anticipated we would. I am grateful to Mimi for enduring these trips, and for everything else.

INTRODUCTION

Presidential Decisions

A few weeks before the US Senate rejected his plan for interstate highway expansion on May 25, 1955, President Dwight Eisenhower wrote to his friend Paul Hoy Helms about his growing frustration with Congress: "Being something of an impatient man, you can imagine the state of my blood pressure when I find measures, obviously designed for the welfare and advancement of the whole country, blocked by partisanship and selfish personal reasons."[1]

For a man who had long endured poor health, who for years had smoked several packs of cigarettes a day, and who would go on to suffer a heart attack in September 1955, Eisenhower's comment about his blood pressure signaled more than mere impatience with the legislative process.[2] At the time of his letter to Helms, Eisenhower had been working with members of his administration on a plan to overhaul the US highway system since early 1953— for more than two years. During that period, Eisenhower had created four different study groups to examine highway expansion, three of which had produced nothing of consequence. He had witnessed the Republicans lose their majorities in both houses of Congress in the 1954 midterms. He had seen his administration's bill received with hostility and incredulity by Democrats in the House and the Senate. And on March 28, 1955, the president had learned that his recent appointee for comptroller general had testified against his own administration's highway bill before the Senate Subcommittee on Roads, effectively dooming the already jeopardized legislation.

Finally, on July 27, 1955, just before Congress concluded that year's session, the House voted 292–123 against a highway expansion bill, and it seemed to everyone involved that Eisenhower's push for significant highway legislation had ended in miserable failure. When asked about the odds that significant highway legislation would pass when Congress reconvened in 1956, Republican congressman and Eisenhower ally George Dondero replied, "If I had to bet on it, I wouldn't use my own money."[3]

Dondero would have been wise to take the bet, and to use his own money. A year later, the House passed a massive highway bill 388–19 on April 27, 1956, and the Senate also passed a similar bill with an 89–1 vote one month later. On July 29, 1956, from his hospital bed at the Walter Reed Army Medical Center, President Eisenhower signed into law the National Interstate and Defense Highways Act: the largest infrastructure project in US history.

This book is an analysis of the decisions Eisenhower made to support federal highway expansion during his first term as president. Specifically, it is an analysis of the decisions he made, over the course of roughly three and a half years, about how to navigate the political and administrative hurdles that stood in the way of significant highway legislation. What does it mean to analyze this kind of presidential decision?

US presidents do not decide whether bills become laws, and the question of what political matters, if any, presidents can actually decide for themselves is itself contested.[4] At the very least, persuading both houses of Congress to pass a bill never simply comes down to a president's decision. Presidents can decide how to attempt to control and influence the process by which legislation makes its way through Congress. They can decide whom to put in charge of developing policy; how to negotiate with members of their own and the opposing party; how to pitch a legislative proposal to the public; and with whom to coordinate in the House and the Senate. They can also decide on the general strategy that they will attempt to follow in the course of advocating for legislation over time. But they cannot simply decide whether a bill will become law.

As an analysis of a landmark presidential decision—Eisenhower's decision to support interstate highway expansion—this book has two interrelated purposes. The first is to identify the most important considerations that were on Eisenhower's mind as he advocated for federal highway expansion, and to consider how the tactical and organizational decisions he made to pursue that goal relate to his broader decision to support highway expansion in the first place. Its second purpose is to probe the relationship between the major decisions Eisenhower made about how to steer his legislative proposal through the legislative process, and how that process unfolded in the White House, in the federal bureaucracy, and in Congress. In what ways and to what extent did Eisenhower's decisions actually influence the legislative process that culminated in the Highway Act of 1956?

Eisenhower's role in federal highway expansion is a particularly helpful case for reflecting on the general theme of presidential decisions for two reasons. First, his decision was a complex one. There was no single factor (e.g., an economic incentive or a psychological impulse) that clearly determined his conduct. Ike made decisions relating to highway expansion in reference to a complex network of considerations, and understanding why he made the decisions he did requires delineating the internal hierarchy of those considerations. We must balance his own professed reasons for deciding how he did—the rationales he elaborated both in public and in private—alongside the motivations that we suspect to have influenced his decisions based on inferences drawn from his conduct.

Second, Eisenhower's decision is a helpful case because his reasons evolved over time—in part because of changes in his political landscape, and in part because of changes in his understanding of the immense undertaking that constituted highway expansion. It is frequently cited, for example, that Eisenhower was impressed by the German national highway system—the *Autobahn*—during World War II, and that these impressions bear significant responsibility for his decision to press for highway expansion in the United States once he became president.[5] It is also frequently alleged that his main preoccupation in 1956 was not with transportation or the economy, but with national defense, and that he viewed interstate highways principally in light of the emerging Soviet military threat. As I will try to show, familiar anecdotes like these tend to obscure, through oversimplification, the numerous goals and influences that competed for attention in Eisenhower's mind as he planned, and then attempted to realize, highway legislation. These included Ike's fear of unemployment and inflation born of a postwar economic recession, his concern with the outcome of the 1954 midterms, and his exposure to business and industrial elites in the years after World War II—elites whose distinctive outlook on politics and economics appears to have influenced his own. More deeply, Eisenhower developed and articulated philosophical reasons (in addition to tactical and strategic ones) to justify his commitment to highway expansion. His experience with

German highways was significant, not simply because it made him want to imitate the German model of transportation, but because it helped him see why certain public undertakings require, by their very nature, centralized funding and planning, and that the traditional American veneration of localized initiative, in this case, therefore stood in the way of the common good.[6] Most deeply, he reflected on the common good of the United States and tried to distinguish his own understanding from alternatives that favored localism and states' rights and that rejected national union and central planning.

It is far from obvious the extent to which the decisions Ike himself made actually advanced the broader enterprise of highway expansion during 1953–1956. The difficulty of answering this question has been enhanced by the accretion of historical myths about his supposedly decisive and single-handed leadership of highway expansion—a myth that has been sustained and perpetuated by the very name the US Federal Highway System was eventually given: the "Dwight D. Eisenhower National System of Interstate and Defense Highways."[7] Unfortunately, the most accurate and in-depth scholarship on this subject tends to be the least well-known to a political science audience; this work has been written not from the standpoint of the presidency but from the perspective of the history and development of transportation in the United States.[8] As for works that do explicitly treat Eisenhower's role in highway expansion, the myth of his outsized leadership role has gained strength as a consequence of imprecise scholarship.

A clear example of this kind of treatment is Stephen Ambrose's account of the Eisenhower presidency, which served as an authoritative account of that subject for more than a generation. Ambrose's discussion of the passage of the 1956 Highway Act gives little indication of the difficulty Eisenhower had in dealing with Congress and members of his own administration. At one point, Ambrose asserts that in 1955, Ike's proposed bill included provisions for a "Highway Trust Fund" and that it "passed the Senate, but it died in the House, where Democrats objected to the bond issue and wanted to instead increase taxes on the trucking industry."[9] This description contains two basic factual errors. First, the Eisenhower bill did not provide for a Highway Trust Fund; instead, it proposed a new government corporation that would have been permitted to borrow funds that technically would not have counted against the federal debt. The latter proposal was ridiculed in Congress and was even criticized by members of Eisenhower's own administration. The Highway Trust Fund Ambrose is referring to was a feature, not of Eisenhower's plan, but of a Democratic bill that would eventually pass Congress in 1956—a bill Eisenhower frequently objected to. Second, Eisenhower's bill never passed the Senate. In fact, it never came close to passing either house of Congress. On May 25, 1955, the Senate voted down the Eisenhower-sponsored bill 60–31. Shortly thereafter on the same day, the Senate approved by voice vote—a procedural indication of the bill's overwhelming popularity in the chamber—a Democratic highway bill, authored by Senator Albert Gore Sr. (D-Tenn.), that was entirely different from Eisenhower's. Later that summer, the House did vote down a highway bill on account of the taxes it proposed to raise. But the bill it rejected had been authored not by the Eisenhower administration but by Democratic representative George Fallon. As in the Senate, the Eisenhower bill never received serious consideration in the House, and the bill that eventually passed both chambers was a synthesis of two separate bills authored by Democrats.[10]

In a similar vein, Eisenhower's most recent biographer, Jean Edward Smith, asserts that "Eisenhower is personally responsible for the interstate highway system."[11] This assertion is misleading on a number of levels. Consider that by 1956 there was overwhelming support in both parties, and at all levels of the states and society, for dramatic federal highway expansion. In fact, support had been growing for more than half a century since the Good Roads Movement of 1880s and 1890s, first popularized by cyclists and later advocated by personal and commercial motorists. What made Eisenhower's intervention into highway politics novel was not his commitment to highway expansion—a lot of people had favored this for a long time before he appeared on the scene[12]—but the particular manner in which he, following the advice of his advisors and committees, proposed funding highway expansion. For it was this question, regarding the financial means by which federal highways were to be expanded—Who would actually pay for this massive undertaking?—that had bedeviled significant progress in the area of federal highway building since the late nineteenth century.[13]

This aspect of highway politics is confirmed by the fact that both of the mechanisms Eisenhower would go on to propose for funding expanded highway construction—toll fees and a government corporation that would issue bonds—never garnered serious support in Congress, where his proposal for a government corporation was voted down twice in under a year. Indeed, the funding mechanism that was eventually agreed upon and signed into law was worked out by congressional Democrats, specifically George Fallon and Hale Boggs in the House of Representatives, and Albert Gore Sr. in the Senate. For his part, Eisenhower and his staff attempted to disrupt progress of the Democratic plan, and in the end the president would express only muted support of the Democratic bill that passed Congress. Eisenhower may have signaled support for highway expansion early and often, and he may have made some decisions that advanced that cause. But it is misleading to allege that he bears "personal responsibility" for it. It is equally mistaken to say that highway expansion happened because of Eisenhower's efforts or in spite of them. Eisenhower's decisions to support highway expansion were some of the numerous (and often mutually competing) influences on the constitutional process that resulted in the 1956 Highway Act. The purpose of this book is to disentangle both the motivations that precipitated Eisenhower's decisions and the ways his decisions interacted with the legislative and administrative process.

Some presidents are able to control every step of the legislative process and obtain a policy outcome that closely, even exactly, resembles the one they envisioned from the start. Perhaps the paradigmatic example of this kind of presidential leadership, for better or worse, is Lyndon Johnson's passage of the Great Society programs.[14] In the case of federal highway expansion, Eisenhower emphatically did not exercise this kind of leadership. Ike instructed his cabinet to begin developing plans for highway expansion less than ten months before the 1954 midterm elections, at which point it was far from certain whether the Republicans would retain their majorities in Congress, and whether the president would therefore be working with Republicans or Democrats. As it happens, the Republicans lost both chambers, likely in part because Eisenhower refused to campaign for Republicans until it was too late.[15] Because the GOP lost its congressional majorities, Ike and his officials were compelled to interact with Democrats who took charge of all the relevant committees in January 1955.

Eisenhower also twice created twin study groups to generate plans for highway expansion—first in April 1954, then in August 1954—and in both cases, the committees lacked a clear sense of their own authority and jurisdiction over the subject matter, which resulted in protracted disagreements and turf wars between them. The plan for highway expansion that the Eisenhower administration did eventually settle on—largely the brainchild of General Lucius Clay, one of the president's most trusted advisors—was publicly criticized by none other than Eisenhower's own appointed comptroller general, Joseph Campbell. Subsequently, the plan was rejected by bipartisan majorities in both houses of Congress in early 1955—and then again in early 1956, after Eisenhower simply resubmitted the original plan that had been rejected the previous year. Finally, the funding plan Congress actually passed in the summer of 1956 bore no resemblance whatsoever to the Clay Committee's funding plan, which Eisenhower had personally endorsed.

For all of these reasons, the process by which Eisenhower attempted to shape interstate highway reform during 1953–1956 serves to complicate Fred Greenstein's well-known reinterpretation of Eisenhower as a shrewd political strategist.[16] Irrespective of other legislative strategies Eisenhower managed to execute successfully—Greenstein does not discuss Ike's leadership of highway expansion—his strategy for highway reform often appears less than sophisticated. Assuming I am able to demonstrate this last point persuasively—this is one of the basic tasks of the book—how should we think about Eisenhower's leadership style and the various ways he chose to interact with constraints imposed by Congress, the White House, and the federal bureaucracy?

Eisenhower is frequently described as respecting the separation of powers. In the words of Stephen Hess, a former Eisenhower administration official, "most presidents spend their years in office pushing against the constitutional wall that separates Article II, Executive Powers, from Article I, Legislative Powers. . . . But this was not Ike's way. He had a strong sense of what belonged to the President and what belonged to Congress."[17] As I will try to show in reference to Eisenhower's strategy for highway reform, this characterization only makes sense if we assume a highly simplistic understanding of what separation of powers is. It is true, as characterizations like these suggest, that Eisenhower largely refused to involve himself with members of Congress in the manner of Franklin Roosevelt, Harry Truman, and LBJ in order to secure passage of his preferred legislation. For Eisenhower, and scholars who characterize him in the above-described way, respecting the separation of powers requires that the president send Congress legislation that he wants and expects them to pass, but without engaging in direct negotiations with members of Congress in order to make passage of those pieces of legislation more likely. This conception of separation of powers assumes that negotiating with members of Congress is a distinctly "legislative" class of activity, and that presidents should therefore refrain from participating in it. Perversely, however, this conception ends up sanctioning the very kinds of behaviors that the separation of powers is intended to proscribe. For a variety of personality-related reasons, Eisenhower disliked direct negotiations with members of Congress, and he justified this aversion on the basis of a constitutional doctrine that he appears to have genuinely believed in. But he also had ideas—often, quite specific ideas—about what kinds of laws he wanted passed. Contrary to the impression one might be left with on the basis of accounts such as Hess's, Eisenhower was not satisfied with allowing Congress to draft bills that he would passively veto or sign; an ambitious and opinionated man, he wanted *his* ideas to become law.

In the case of highway legislation, what this posture incentivized in practice was an almost obsessively executive branch–centered legislative process. Like other characteristically "modern" presidents that preceded and followed him, Eisenhower created a highway bill entirely within the confines of the White House and the Executive Office, using personnel from his administration as well as friends and acquaintances from the military and the private sector, without any congressional involvement whatsoever.[18] This finished bill Eisenhower then presented to the Congress, and he expected the two houses to simply acquiesce to his preferred bill. When his bill was laughed out of the House and the Senate, he was indignant, as the anecdote that opens this chapter confirms.

Eisenhower's particular take on the separation of powers induced him to attempt to supplant Congress's distinctly legislative role—the role it was designed to perform as an institution—by means of the White House and the executive branch. Legislatures are designed to perform a function that executives are ill-equipped to handle, namely, to bring a range of competing interests and perspectives to bear on questions of public policy. The rationale for designing such an institution is that legislation worked out through a process of painstaking negotiation by elected representatives will be inclusive of a broad range of needs and concerns, and that it will approximate the consent of the whole community and not just one part. For this reason, I argue that by shutting out Congress from his legislative process and reassigning that process to members of his administration and people in the business sector, who, in turn, operated in secrecy, Eisenhower was subverting the separation of powers system in the misguided belief that he was honoring it. By drafting legislation behind closed doors within the White House, he was performing a poor imitation of what Congress was actually designed to do as an institution; his administration was, in effect, functioning as a miniature legislature that had none of the procedures, norms, and institutional memory that enabled the actual Congress to perform its task. This process led Eisenhower to approach Congress with a fully worked-out piece of legislation, which he expected to be voted up or down, instead of soliciting their input on and inviting them to negotiate over a set of general legislative principles. Legislators who otherwise might have been inclined to support an administration-backed highway plan nevertheless had their own ideas about highway policy, and were therefore disinclined to support Eisenhower's highway bill; they bristled at the notion of being forced to vote on a concrete proposal without having been involved in its drafting at all. And because Eisenhower was reluctant to negotiate directly with members of Congress before submitting his legislation to each chamber, his highway bill was rebuffed by the House and the Senate, who preferred to draft their own legislation.

Ironically, Eisenhower's misguided view of separation of powers led him to do things he was reluctant and ill-prepared to do. Desiring to pass his preferred programs without having to involve Congress as to their substance, at the last minute the president decided to campaign on behalf of congressional Republicans in the 1954 midterms, despite having resisted those who had been urging him to campaign earlier in the year. He finally acquiesced in large measure because he wanted a unified partisan "team" in charge of both branches of government. That "team," he argued in his campaign speeches, would enable him to send bills to Congress that would be passed as a matter of course. Far from respecting the separation of powers, Eisenhower wanted to combine the separated powers of Congress and the presidency into a single legislative conveyor belt, with his own product simply receiving Congress's rubber stamp at the end of the process.

Notwithstanding these setbacks, landmark highway legislation was passed in 1956, and Eisenhower played a significant (but, as I will argue, a much misunderstood) role in the process that culminated in that legislation. In the chapters that follow, I try to identify the most important decisions Eisenhower made in his yearslong effort to secure passage of a transformative highway program. Through archival research, I also describe in as much detail as possible the background considerations that preceded each of Eisenhower's major decisions, and the ways his decisions interacted with the broader legislative and policymaking process. Accordingly, chapter 1 sketches the history of US federal roadbuilding efforts up to the point of Eisenhower's inauguration in 1953, and his own personal background insofar as it is relevant to his interest in federal highways. Chapter 2 disentangles Ike's early efforts—from 1952 to 1954—to begin formulating a new highway policy, and chapter 3 discusses his decision to form the Clay Committee and the consequences of that decision for his cabinet and his administration as a whole. Chapter 4 examines the failure of the Clay Committee's plan and the role played by congressional leaders during 1955. Chapter 5 describes and considers the reasons for congressional defeat in the summer of 1955 and then congressional victory a year later. My conclusion discusses some of the takeaways that presidential scholars with different backgrounds and methodological assumptions might draw from Eisenhower's experience with federal highway expansion.

CHAPTER 1

Background and Context, 1787–1952

When Dwight Eisenhower began advocating for highway expansion early in his first presidential term, he brought with him his own history and character—the tastes, habits, and idiosyncrasies that shaped the way he interacted with other members of the federal government and that influenced his overall decision-making process. In addition to these internal influences, Eisenhower also confronted a tangled web of interests around federal highway policy, a web that was the inheritance of the complex development of roadway politics in the United States. Before turning to the decisions he actually made as president, this chapter will briefly consider the effects that both of these sets of influences likely had on Eisenhower as he approached the question of highway expansion. My goal is not to demonstrate that certain preexisting psychological or institutional forces necessitated the actions he undertook, but rather to tease out some of the most important behavioral patterns he exhibited going into his presidency, and to delineate the particular challenges that highway politics would have posed for any president in his position. In turn, these considerations can inform and contextualize our analysis of the concrete steps Ike took to promote highway reform.

US Federal Highways before the Modern Era

When the United States became a sovereign nation in the late eighteenth century, other relatively developed countries had established roadbuilding traditions dating back centuries. But unlike in most European nations, where political authority was relatively centralized and where roadbuilding could therefore be executed in a uniform way, authority in the United States was originally dispersed between the states and localities, with the national government having only weak and limited administrative capacities.[1] This political arrangement was an inheritance from the American colonial era, during which "roadmaking and mending were responsibilities of the local governments."[2] Starting with the ratification of the new constitution in 1788, the states became more involved in roadbuilding in response to local demands, but even these efforts were minimal, and the federal government initially had almost nothing to do with public roads.[3] Moreover, divided political authority in the early American republic compounded all of the difficulties that are inherent to the very enterprise of roadbuilding. Not only did the states have to allocate scarce resources in a mutually satisfactory way between competing parts of the community, but there also existed multiple hierarchies within the states themselves: the federal government, state governments, and localities. And where authority was located within these mutually suspicious, sometimes openly hostile, hierarchies was often far from clear. For these reasons, early efforts by the federal government to construct highways to ease travel between the states were rebuffed by those within the states who saw federal roadbuilding as an encroachment on their authority.

Roadbuilding efforts fared better within the states themselves, where political power was more consolidated during the early nineteenth century.[4] Privately run toll road companies used their influence with state legislatures to obtain contracts to build roads and highways paid for by user fees.[5] However, even these efforts were frequently hamstrung by the decentralized character of decision-making authority in the broader regime. Construction and administration of roads "varied widely from company to company," and a lack of coordination meant that routes were often haphazardly and incoherently drawn.[6] Finally, state roadbuilding programs were undermined by, and eventually collapsed as a consequence of, the rapid rise of railroads, which rendered slow overland travel by means of horse and wagon obsolete.[7]

Roadbuilding did not become a priority again until the rise of bicycles in the late nineteenth century and, much more significantly, the introduction of the automobile in the early twentieth. However, the federal government still had little incentive to rock the legislative boat until automobile users began to organize nationally, a process that was rendered especially difficult given the country's physical scale and the ever-present problem of free riding. Nevertheless, starting in the 1880s, members of what would come to be called the "Good Roads Movement" began pressuring Congress to take national action, and in 1883, the first state road convention was held in Iowa City, Iowa.[8] Congress began to respond around this time, albeit tentatively and cautiously, with one chamber occasionally passing a highway bill that the other would vote down or ignore. When Congress finally created the Office of Road Inquiry within the Department of Agriculture in 1893, the purpose of that organization was only to explore the possibility of future roadbuilding projects, not to actually build highways. Congress did not formally appropriate money for roadbuilding projects until 1916, with the passage of the first Federal-Aid Highway Act signed into law by Woodrow Wilson. The act authorized $25 million annually, but the logic of the legislation was decidedly state-centric.[9] Instead of the federal government planning and building routes, the states proposed their own highway plans, which the federal government would consider, and usually approve. Further, no aid could be given to a state unless its legislature approved the plan. It was also the responsibility of the states to maintain federal-aid roads once they had been built, which meant that states could allow interstate routes to fall into disrepair, and there was nothing the federal government could do about it. And because states had to match federal funds, even poor states that wanted to launch ambitious roadbuilding projects nevertheless received less federal money and, consequently, built fewer roads.[10]

In the four decades that followed the 1916 act, federal roadbuilding went slowly for the reasons described above. States continued to guard their roadbuilding prerogatives out of twin fears that a federal program would place routes where states and local communities did not want them, and that any federal tax burden for funding highways would be born inequitably by states that differed significantly in population and landmass. In these struggles, states were abetted by the new head of federal roadbuilding efforts, Thomas Harris MacDonald. In 1918, the Office of Public Roads—the successor to the Office of Road Inquiry—was elevated to the status of "Bureau" within the Department of Agriculture, where it would stay for another two decades. The following year, the new Bureau of Public Roads (BPR) was put in the charge of MacDonald, a well-known highway engineer from Iowa. As a state highway official, MacDonald developed and retained a state-centric view of highway matters even after he assumed his new federal position. Within the state highway universe, MacDonald had earned overwhelming respect, and Woodrow Wilson appointed him in part because he had received "the unanimous recommendations of the American Association of State Highway Officials."[11] However, if Wilson had hoped for a BPR director, in MacDonald, who would be open to greater federal coordination and planning of public roads, he was to be sorely mistaken. Besides his technical competence as an engineer, MacDonald appears to have gained the support of state highway officials because he embodied what they all had in common, namely, deep-seated hostility toward federal involvement in highway policy. Indeed, MacDonald was a creature of the very world that had held back federal highway expansion during the early twentieth century and that had only grudgingly accommodated it in the decades that followed. Time and again, MacDonald demonstrated his commitment to the authority of individual states over and against the needs of the fast-growing nation.[12]

In addition to MacDonald's recalcitrance, two world wars did not help highway matters; they diverted money, supplies, and labor that would normally have been available for highway construction. On this score, the moment that seemed most propitious for finally expanding federal highways came during the early New Deal, when the federal government was eagerly looking for ways to employ millions of citizens who had been ruined by the Great Depression.[13] Make-work projects such as the Civilian Conservation Corps (CCC) suggested an avenue for finally solving a public works problem that was intensifying as more Americans than ever owned and drove automobiles. But before work could begin in earnest, the United States entered World War II, and roadbuilding once again came to a halt for want of supplies and workers.[14]

After the war, the combination of returning soldiers and an exponentially growing automobile industry—car construction had halted during the war—made apparent the urgent need for highway construction. And yet, the institutional pathways that had developed around roadbuilding in the United States during the nineteenth and early twentieth centuries continued to frustrate all but the most minimalistic attempts at progress. Congress continued to reauthorize the Federal-Aid Act every two years, and even commissioned the BPR to plan 40,000 miles of routes for future highway construction.[15] But because the Federal-Aid Act only authorized a few hundred million dollars for highway maintenance over two years, the federal government had no hope of undertaking the kind of highway overhaul that was desperately needed without a massive influx of funds. For these reasons, during the late 1940s and early 1950s it was easier—at the political level, at least—to simply muddle on with inadequate roads than to champion a new roadbuilding project that would require everyone to sacrifice something.

Broadly stated, then, the options on the table when Eisenhower was elected president in 1952 were (1) to retain the status quo; (2) to expand on but not fundamentally alter the status quo, perhaps by increasing overall federal funding or raising the federal matching rate to incentivize more state construction projects; or (3) to overhaul the system entirely and create a centrally planned, centrally regulated federal interstate network.

Dwight Eisenhower and Interstate Highways

Dwight David Eisenhower was born in Denison, Texas, on October 14, 1890, and spent most of his early years in Abilene, Kansas. He attended the US Military Academy at West Point, where he graduated in 1915. Despite his frequent requests, he did not see combat action in Europe in World War I, instead serving as a tank crew commander at several different US Army bases throughout the United States. In the decades following World War I, Eisenhower gradually rose through the ranks and served as aide to prominent generals, including Douglas MacArthur and George Marshall. In 1919, he participated in a cross-country US Army convoy intended by President Wilson to showcase the inadequacy of the country's roadways.[16] During the early years of World War II, he worked closely with Marshall, who promoted him rapidly.

Eisenhower commanded the invasion of North Africa in 1942 and, in December 1943, President Roosevelt chose Eisenhower over Marshall to be Supreme Allied Commander of the invasion of Europe. Following the war, he served as US Army chief of staff and the supreme commander of NATO; between these two positions, he also served as president of Columbia University. Despite not having publicly affiliated himself with either political party, Eisenhower was recruited by Republican elites to run for president in 1952. He served two full terms, defeating Democratic nominee Adlai Stevenson twice, in 1952 and 1956. He was the first Republican president to serve in twenty years.

What kinds of ideas and experiences are likely to have shaped Eisenhower's approach to highway expansion? As far as his political philosophy is concerned, Ike was by no means a systematic political thinker, even by the standards of politicians. Over the course of his life, he occasionally expressed affinity for different political movements and leaders: for example, he favored a strong presidency on the model of Franklin Roosevelt during the early years of the New Deal, when legislative inaction seemed to threaten the state's ability to respond to fascism and communism abroad.[17] Relatedly, study of his private writings and correspondences during and immediately following his service in World War II suggests that Eisenhower regarded excessive nationalism and parochialism as a hindrance to economic development and political stability. He was open to and even enthusiastic about globalization in the form of multilateral organizations such as NATO and the United Nations, free trade, and immigration, going so far as to state in his 1953 State of Union message that a priority of his administration would be "to foster the advent of practical unity in Western Europe," a comment that clearly presaged the European Union.[18] At a preinaugural meeting with his future cabinet on January 12, 1953, he stated—to the consternation of the more hardline anticommunists in the group—"I have a very deep conviction that there is no instrument in the hands of diplomacy that is quite as powerful as trade."[19] Accordingly, early in his administration he pushed to renew a free trade policy, put in place by the Democrats in 1934, that significantly reduced tariffs on foreign manufactured products: "Eisenhower had a theoretical commitment to free trade."[20] Breaking with traditional elements within the Republican Party, he favored China's participation in the newly established UN and, guarding presidential prerogatives that had been exercised by internationalist Democrats Roosevelt and Truman, he opposed the conservative Bricker Amendment that would have constrained the president's ability to negotiate international agreements for the whole country.[21]

Eisenhower was by no means philosophically coherent on any of these points. As we will see in chapters 3 and 4, he was perfectly willing to abandon his 1952 campaign promise to be committed to "fiscal responsibility" and balanced budgets when he thought he could get away with it. Nevertheless, Eisenhower's openness to interstate highway expansion, a project that would put many still disparate parts of the United States into direct contact with each other, and contribute to the growth and stability of the US economy, was doubtless rooted in his broader ideas about political coherence and economic development—ideas that he frequently referred to as "Progressive Republicanism," a label he used to distinguish himself from conservative Republicans.[22] These ideas are reflected in his administration's highway message to Congress in 1955: "Our unity as a nation is sustained by free communication of thought and by easy transportation of people and goods.... Together, the uniting forces of our communication and transportation systems are dynamic elements in the very name we bear—United States. Without them, we would be a mere alliance of many separate parts."[23]

In addition to the political ideas he held regarding these various aspects of public policy, Eisenhower had an acute and outwardly noticeable affinity for business and industrial leaders, an affinity that he exhibited starting with his retirement from the US Army following the end of the war. In the chapters that follow, I will refer to this phenomenon as Eisenhower's period of "elite socialization."

Following his retirement, Ike was approached by leading industry and business figures in the United States who sought to befriend him and to ingratiate themselves with the now-famous war hero, and whose efforts culminated in their successful attempt to recruit him for the presidency in 1952.[24] In turn, Eisenhower promised these friends that, if elected, he would be committed to rolling back New Deal policies that had been unfriendly to big business and industry.[25] And by the time he decided to run for president, "there was scarcely a successful businessman, publisher, or financier in the country who had not experienced Eisenhower's firm handshake."[26] Starting in 1948, he gave frequent talks at elite economic venues, such as investors' meetings, banks, the New York Racquet Club, and Standard Oil headquarters.[27] After he was elected with their help, these new friends eventually constituted a small group whom Eisenhower affectionately referred to as "the gang."[28] Among them were "William Robinson, *New York Herald Tribune* executive and later president of Coca-Cola; Ellis D. Slater, president of Frankfort Distillers; Clifford Roberts, an investment banker and Augusta National Golf Club chairman; W. Alton Jones, head of the Cities Service oil company (now Citgo); and George E. Allen, a lawyer-financier-lobbyist."[29] Eisenhower frequently met with these men and solicited their advice, usually while golfing: "Following his elections, his gang got together and agreed that they would always be available to the President whenever he had a free moment for golf and bridge . . . they felt they had played a major role in convincing their friend to take on the Presidency."[30] For his part, Eisenhower allowed "the gang" to buy him expensive gifts, including cattle for his ranch near Gettysburg, Pennsylvania, and a house on the Augusta National Golf Course.[31] "He sought their advice on politics, economics, and finance, both in general and with regard to his personal fortunes. He accepted from them many gifts, services, free trips, etc.," Ambrose states.[32] And, most importantly for our purposes, he involved them directly with policymaking and asked them to draft legislation. "With them," notes Ambrose, "[Eisenhower] could discuss politics or economics or statecraft seriously. Whatever his mood, the gang adjusted to it, because the members were devoted to him."[33]

Establishing what motivated "the gang" to befriend Eisenhower in this way is not within the scope of this book. Doubtless it was a complex mixture of genuine affection and a desire to influence the president in a way that benefited them personally and professionally. From the standpoint of analyzing Eisenhower's decision-making process, the more relevant question is the reverse: What attracted Eisenhower to these men, and to what extent did different kinds of exposure to them shape the political choices he made as president? Historian Michael Beschloss observes that "after V-E Day [Eisenhower] was susceptible to the allure of the financial power elite. Having grown up on what was considered the wrong side of the tracks in Abilene, Kan., he clearly enjoyed being around such moguls."[34] On this point, contemporaneous commentators on the political Left frequently suspected the undue influence of industry over the Eisenhower administration, a suspicion that gained in credibility after he appointed a cadre of bankers and corporate executives to his cabinet. As newspapers pointed out in discussing those appointments, the group was marked by inexperience in government and an overrepresentation of business and industry, with the *New Republic* calling the president's cabinet "eight millionaires and one plumber."[35] In 1959, Senator John Kennedy stated that "he would have expected Eisenhower, the World War II hero, to be playing golf with his old Army friends, but carped that 'all his golfing pals are rich men he has met since 1945.'"[36]

Eisenhower seems to have genuinely admired business and industry leaders as a consequence of his frustration with the relentlessly bureaucratic structure and operations of the US military. He appreciated the relative freedom and unconstrained creativity that life in the private sector permitted and incentivized: "Always impressed by successful businessmen who had made it on their own and who knew how to run huge organizations, [Eisenhower] sought out the high achievers, men he could turn to for advice and with whom he could share both responsibility and praise."[37] He felt similar frustrations with the elites who had come to serve as the leaders of the New Deal. In his private diary, Eisenhower wrote that unless he could choose whom to put in as top administration officials, "sooner or later we will be unable to get anybody to take jobs in Washington except business failures, college professors, and New Deal lawyers. All of these would jump at the chance to get a job that a successful businessman has to sacrifice very much to take."[38] Did it occur to Eisenhower that business elites were not necessarily sacrificing their own interests by taking a government position—indeed, that they might use government influence to help their interests? Secretary of Defense Charles Wilson was head of General Motors, which held $3 billion in defense contracts.[39] Directly relevant to the subject of this book, the man Eisenhower asked to write highway legislation in 1954, General Lucius Clay, drafted a highway plan that would have paid more than $11 billion in taxpayer dollars to interest payments for a bond issue.

Many of those who stood to benefit most from the proposed bonds—leading bankers and Wall Street financiers—had, in various ways, also been involved in the bill's drafting. Perhaps aware of how these decisions might be perceived as signaling undue influence, Eisenhower was defensive of them. He insisted in his memoirs, "Every one of [the gang] made it a matter of personal honor to avoid any attempt to influence a governmental policy or official by reason of close association with me. These were men of discretion, men who, already successful, made no attempt to profit by our association."[40]

Questions of overt impropriety aside, it remains an undeniable fact that Eisenhower surrounded himself in a very particular demographic during his presidency—business and industrial elites—and that his decision to associate with them so constantly had the effect of limiting the kind of political advice and feedback he was likely to receive: "Eisenhower might have developed a wider understanding of the human experience had his inner circle been more diverse."[41] It likely did not help matters that Eisenhower's favorite news source was the *Chicago Herald-Tribune*, whose editor, Robert McCormick, was a hardline conservative within the world of Republican politics.[42] Personally, Eisenhower was free to make up his own mind about political matters, but the company he chose to keep had concrete political and economic goals they had been pursuing for most of their lives. At the very least, Eisenhower appears to have been sympathetic to these goals and to have believed that leaders of the private sector brought certain virtues to the work of government that those who had been given authority under the New Deal lacked. In practice, as we will see, this meant outsourcing the development of his administration's interstate highway program to members of the private sector who had concrete ideas of their own about good public policy and who were frequently baffled by the operations of the federal government.

CHAPTER 2

Presidential Initiative

Eisenhower's Initial Forays into Highway Expansion, 1952–1954

> *Eisenhower is not taking government out of business, he is giving government to business.*
> —*The New Republic*, December 1, 1952

When President Eisenhower met with congressional Republicans at the beginning of his first term, on February 9, 1953, highway expansion was not on the legislative agenda.[1] Nor did Eisenhower mention highway expansion during his first State of the Union Address, delivered the previous week.[2] Yet during the preceding months, Ike had been taking deliberate steps toward devising a plan for highway expansion. Before taking office, Eisenhower released a public statement to the Hearst newspapers emphatically endorsing the idea of highway expansion.[3] In that statement, he emphasized the negative effects that the current highway system was imposing on the country. He also observed that expanded roadways would provide positive benefits to the economy and society: "New roads to meet the requirements of today and the foreseeable future ... will be a foundation for the progress ahead," and "modern roads are necessary to defense."

There was nothing unusual about a president endorsing the idea of highway expansion. And given the traditional relationship that had been developed between the federal government and states and counties since the creation of the Bureau of Public Roads (BPR) and the earliest Federal-Aid Acts, Eisenhower's rhetorical show of deference to local communities is unsurprising. Notwithstanding this explicit criticism of the logic of New Deal governance, however, Eisenhower also asserted in his Hearst statement that "the national government can supply leadership of the kind that is lacking today." What precise form this kind of leadership would have to take, Eisenhower did not mention—an understandable choice, given the difficulties that previous presidents had encountered in attempting to create a larger role for the federal government in highway politics. Yet Eisenhower was also quiet, if not perfectly silent, about the tradeoffs and hard decisions that would have to be made if significant highway legislation were to become a reality. How is "national leadership," which Eisenhower clearly viewed as both lacking and necessary, to be reconciled with the autonomy of local communities, which Eisenhower evidently regarded as having been violated by the nationalizing policies of his two immediate predecessors? Clearly, at this stage in his planning, either Eisenhower was unaware of the hard questions that his self-proclaimed "crusade" would require answering or he preferred to speak at a level of abstraction that enabled him to leave those questions unarticulated.

How Eisenhower would answer those questions started to become more apparent in the months following his inauguration. In early 1953, Ike commissioned Wall Street investor Walker G. Buckner to prepare "an outline study ... on the general subject of building a highway system in the United States as a series of self-liquidating projects."[4] Buckner worked at Reynolds & Co. of New York, a real estate and private equity firm.[5] During the first week of February, Buckner submitted his plan to the White House, and on February 4, 1953, he met with the president to discuss it in detail.[6] Buckner's plan established the basic terms of the debate over highway expansion that would unfold within the administration during the next two years. On the first page of his report, Buckner states that the roadbuilding projects he recommends "can be constructed by private enterprise and the funds provided by private capital."[7] Buckner elaborates that "financing, if insured by the Federal Government, would make it possible to raise large amounts of money at substantially reduced costs to the various projects which would be individually too small to advantageously market their bonds." The government could raise enormous amounts of money by guaranteeing repayment of bonds plus interest and by packaging together many different small roadbuilding projects into one massive piece of legislation.

At this point, it seems clear that Buckner was advocating a straightforward bond issue that would add to the national debt while enabling the government to build highways relatively quickly without having to raise taxes. Yet such a proposal would clearly have violated Eisenhower's campaign promise not to increase the country's indebtedness—a promise Buckner was no doubt aware of. Buckner therefore went on to assert that "all projects should be self-supporting and should not increase national indebtedness." How can a highway project depend on bonds and not add to the national debt at the same time? Buckner concluded that "some bankers may have reservations on this point which can be overcome by some form of government insurance." The "reservation" in question would seem to be that, under Buckner's plan, the bonds issued by the government to raise funds for highway construction would somehow not be included in the national debt.

After his meeting with Buckner, Eisenhower forwarded Buckner's plan to Gabriel Hauge, administrative assistant to the president. Eisenhower's penchant for recruiting people not in government for his projects was on display in the case of Hauge. Prior to joining Eisenhower's administration, Hauge, a professor of economics, had served as an economic advisor for 1948 Republican presidential candidate, Thomas Dewey; among other positions, he had been an editor at *Business Week* magazine. After working for Eisenhower, he joined the leadership of the bank holding company Manufacturers Trust.[8] In his memo to Hauge, Eisenhower suggests that he is interested in pursuing highway expansion for a number of reasons. Early on, he mentions the current inadequacy of roads in the United States to growing traffic needs, and the resultant need for more capacious highways.[9] He goes on to indicate that current traffic congestion and related problems are not so urgent as to warrant immediate attention: "This entire subject of vehicular traffic is but a small segment of the great program that must attract our attention." He also proposes undertaking further study of the highway question, "so as to have [a study of the traffic problem] ready for inclusion into a broad plan to be developed later."[10] Near the end of his memo, Eisenhower floats the possibility of developing a plan that could be deployed piecemeal "without completion of the entire plan." His rationale was that discrete roadbuilding programs could "have some effect on leveling out peaks and valleys in our economic life." In other words, his concern was less with developing a comprehensive plan to render the roadways adequate to present and future traffic needs—a project that would seem to require urgency—than with finding ways to use roadbuilding as but one means of mitigating unemployment and related economic problems brought on by a recession or depression.

On the sensitive question of how to pursue "self-liquidating projects," Eisenhower prevaricated. This formulation, which implies a substantial roadbuilding project that will, nevertheless, not require borrowing and resultant additions to the federal deficit, reflects his campaign commitment to fiscal responsibility and his repudiation of New Deal understandings of governmental finance. Further, his allusions to a substantial highway project that would somehow pay for itself presupposed a feat that no previous administration had been able to accomplish. In effect, then, Ike's assignment for Buckner and Hauge was to generate a plan that could thread the needle—namely, an expensive public works project that would require neither budged deficits nor tax increases—that had alluded presidents since Woodrow Wilson.

Hauge forwarded Buckner's report to the Department of Commerce, in which was housed the BPR, still headed by Director Thomas MacDonald. In 1939, the BPR had been moved from Agriculture to the newly created Department of Public Works; when the latter was eliminated in 1949, it was sent to Commerce, where it would remain until the creation of the Department of Transportation in 1967.[11] It is unclear how either MacDonald or newly appointed Commerce Secretary Sinclair Weeks reacted to Buckner's study. However, several months later on May 26, 1953, MacDonald was unceremoniously fired from his position by Weeks and replaced by Francis Victor du Pont. Given Eisenhower's public statement about a departure from former ways of administering federal roads, in addition to his commissioning of a private consultant to develop radical new plans for highway expansion, it is reasonable to infer that MacDonald, head of the federal government's sole roadbuilding authority, had been less than receptive to the new president's initial gestures. MacDonald was the consummate defender both of governmental professionalism and of the prerogatives traditionally maintained by state and local governments in the area of federal highway policy. MacDonald also controlled his department with unusual skill and tenacity. The prospect of a new, federally dominated highway program masterminded by private consultants is therefore unlikely to have appealed to him. By replacing MacDonald with Du Pont, the son of a business tycoon who had once constructed a private highway at his own expense, Eisenhower was sending a signal that the modes of governing and administering federal roads that had become traditional were no longer to be taken for granted.[12]

After several months of inactivity on the highway front, Eisenhower again confronted the tension between roadbuilding and budgetary responsibility on November 5, 1953, in a memorandum to his budget bureau director, Joseph Dodge.[13] As we might expect given his campaign commitment to fiscal responsibility, Eisenhower states in that memo that his administration should publicly take credit for having reduced projected governmental expenditures. He urges Dodge to ensure that agencies continue to distinguish between "necessary" and "desirable" expenses in order to create an ethos of thrift rather than one of indulgence. Yet Ike also acknowledges the inherent difficulty of drawing clear-cut distinctions based on "necessity and desirability," given the differing priorities that different parts of the federal government necessarily place on competing projects and commitments. Eisenhower goes on to elaborate this dilemma by stating that he intends to curb unnecessary expenses, but he also wants to commit his administration to "broad and liberal objectives in certain fields that affect our whole country directly."[14] Specifically, and "to give substance to our words," he states that he "would like to see no reduction—possibly even a slight increase" in appropriations for "a few small public works projects."[15]

Taken together with his previous remarks to subordinates, including Buckner, Hauge, and Lodge, Eisenhower's memorandum to Dodge suggests that the president was entertaining two possible approaches to federal roadbuilding. On the one hand, he was interested in an ambitious project to transform federal highways that would doubtless require statutory authorization; this was the plan he gestured to in his Hearst piece and that he asked Buckner to study. Of course, the challenge posed by such a project would be how to finance it without either raising taxes or adding to the national debt. On the other hand, Eisenhower was clearly distressed by economic instability and, more concretely, by the prospect of a recession or depression that would result in the unemployment of millions of Americans. Federal roadbuilding could have provided employment opportunities in a pinch, and the question would then have been how to choose and finance such opportunities. In his comments to Budget Director Dodge, Eisenhower was considering the feasibility of spending spare funds from the Commerce Department in case of an economic emergency.

Two months after his memorandum to Dodge, in his Annual Message to Congress delivered on January 7, 1954, Eisenhower was conservative in his recommendations regarding highway building. He stated only that the federal government was "continuing its central role in the Federal Highway Program," a statement that committed his administration to nothing new in this policy area.[16] Then, a few weeks after his Annual Message, Eisenhower sent a secret memorandum to the chair of the President's Council of Economic Advisors (CEA), Dr. Arthur Burns, regarding ways to combat and possibly prevent "depression or serious deflation."[17] In his memo, Eisenhower distinguishes between economic measures that could be adopted by the president without congressional authorization and measures such as "alterations in tax laws" and "unemployment insurance programs" that would "require Congressional action."[18] The memo goes on to suggest that public works projects, including roadbuilding, could fit into either of these categories depending on the nature and scope of their financial commitments. To this end, Eisenhower asks Burns to provide him with an outline of the status of public works projects that were either currently in operation or set to initiate in the next budgetary cycle. He also provides Burns with a list of the kinds of projects that might be included in the budget, and one of these is "good road development."

By early 1954, Eisenhower had placed two members of his administration in organizational positions to study interstate highway expansion. However, even though his party held majorities in both chambers of Congress and he was clearly aware that significant highway expansion would require congressional action, Ike had yet to raise the matter with congressional leaders.

In a cabinet meeting on February 5, 1954, Eisenhower raised the issue of implementing a robust public works program for the first time with all the significant members of his administration present. Indeed, according to handwritten notes of the meeting taken by the president's press secretary, James Hagerty, "public works program" was the first and by far the longest discussed item on that day's agenda.[19] In his remarks, Eisenhower noted that he was viewing public works programs, including "road" and "highway programs," from three distinct vantage points. First, they could be used to improve the economy in the short term in case of recession or depression. According to Hagerty, the president stated that there was a "need of getting real [public works] program ready—'level of government work up so that if needed it could be used immediately to put people back to work'—'if we don't move rapidly, we could be in terrible trouble.'" Second, the president "urged road, school, highway programs to improve the welfare of nation." Third, Eisenhower contended that a public works program would help the Republican Party electorally: "If we are actually building more and putting more people back to work, [I] can think of no better effect on Election Day." Indeed, the president anticipated a "tremendous effect in Congress" if the administration were "to actually start some projects right now."[20] On the latter point, Hagerty notes that Treasury Secretary George Humphrey drew the same connection between a public works program and winning "the '54 elections." According to Humphrey, "we must do everything we honorably can to win them."[21]

Despite Ike's sense of urgency—"start some projects *right now*"—and despite the looming 1954 midterm elections, no significant action was taken in the area of public works in the months following the February 5 cabinet meeting. A likely reason that Eisenhower ceased to regard shovel-ready projects with the sense of urgency that had previously possessed him is that the mild economic recession that had set in immediately following demobilization after the Korean War had begun to lift in the first and second quarters of 1954 (see fig. 2.1).

Accordingly, the trajectory of Eisenhower's highway project began to change after the February 5 meeting, as urgency and shovel-ready projects began to lose their relevance. Mark Rose describes the situation well:

> Between January 1953, and early 1954, Eisenhower's top-level officials had failed to agree about the essentials of a remodeled highway program, one actually sufficient for handling the traffic

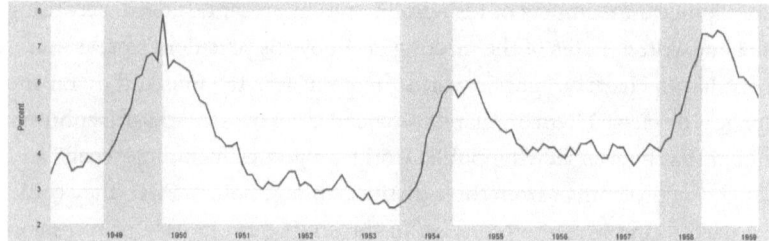

Figure 2.1: Unemployment rose from mid-1953 until early and mid-1954. US recessions are shaded. Source: Graph provided by the Federal Reserve Bank of St. Louis, https://fred.stlouisfed.org/graph/?g=BDMJ.

upsurge and bolstering the economy. That more road building would halt the post–Korean War downturn in the economy seemed reasonable enough to most, but for the specifics of a program all awaited the report of a presidential commission and lobbied for pet schemes.[22]

To Rose's analysis we might add that, by early 1954, it was still unclear to everyone involved—evidently, including Eisenhower himself—whether the chief purpose of embarking on an expansion of federal highways was still to address the post–Korean War recession, as opposed to, say, mitigating traffic fatalities, meeting traffic needs, and expanding the economy in the long term: all purposes the president had, at different moments, articulated. And although he was clearly interested in federal roadbuilding projects, Eisenhower was nonetheless reluctant to even sketch the broad outlines of an actual plan, let alone commit himself to highway expansion in any meaningful way.

A Tale of Two Committees, Part I

During mid-1954, Eisenhower made three important decisions related to highway expansion. First, he abandoned the idea of pursuing small, piecemeal roadbuilding projects in favor of an ambitious new highway program that would transform the US transportation system. Second, he decided to bring the idea of highway expansion out of the White House and the Executive Office—where it had previously been confined—to the public. To advance these goals, he instructed Arthur

Burns and Sherman Adams, his chief of staff, to lead separate groups to study highway expansion.

When Eisenhower forwarded Walker Buckner's plan to Gabriel Hauge on February 4, 1953, Hauge in turn sent the memorandum to key members of the administration who had been, or would become, involved in highway expansion. These included Sinclair Weeks of Commerce, Francis du Pont of the BPR, and General John Stewart Bragdon, a military colleague of Eisenhower's who now worked under Burns at the CEA. From there, Buckner's report made its way to other interested parties, but nothing transpired in the way of concrete action in the months following Buckner's report, notwithstanding the president's occasional comments about roadbuilding and public works programs during 1953 and early 1954.

On December 23, 1953, Assistant Secretary of Commerce for Transportation Robert Murray (who had received Buckner's report from Commerce Secretary Weeks) wrote back to Hauge stating that federal financing of highway expansion of the kind suggested by Buckner was undesirable, and that state and local governments should continue to be the primary financers.[23] At this point, the Commerce Department was clearly uninterested in significant federal highway expansion. Lewis helpfully states, "The conventional conservative wisdom of many in the [Eisenhower] administration, including Secretary of Commerce Sinclair Weeks . . . held that the Federal government should not embark on large-scale public works projects."[24] It is therefore unsurprising that on April 9, 1954, when General Bragdon asked to meet with Murray concerning the 1954 Federal-Aid Bill, "Murray emphasized his highway bill was a regular one which did not give much more to any one State than last year."[25] As for an expanded highway program, he stated that the BPR had sufficient funds for a "supplemental program for Public Works," and that "an emergency public works program should be supplemental." By this, he appears to have meant that Ike's remarks about "a few small public works projects" to Budget Director Dodge back in November 1953 could be met with supplements from existing Department of Commerce funds, but that it should not be pursued through new legislation that would either displace or replace—rather than merely supplement—existing Federal-Aid arrangements.[26]

Bragdon was not going to be stonewalled by Secretary Murray. Bragdon, too, had received Buckner's report from Hauge back in early 1953, and he appears to have been discussing highway policy with Murray principally in order to sound out the rest of Commerce's mood regarding highway expansion. Thus, if his notes of the meeting are accurate, Bragdon did not actually raise the subject of Buckner's report with Murray, but merely gauged his attitude toward the subject in general.

Nevertheless, the conversation clearly provoked Bragdon to take a greater interest in highway expansion. Three days later, he was involved in a sudden flurry of activity concerning highways. During a White House conference that day, Eisenhower stated that he was "interested in self-liquidating projects"—which was, after all, nothing new.[27] What was new was his position that such projects "might require legislation for federal aid in guaranteeing loans." Eisenhower now felt that the government would need to borrow funds to complete highway expansion after all, and that Congress would therefore need to pass legislation authorizing the government to issue bonds to raise those funds. In addition to expressing his continued interest in highway expansion in the form of highway legislation, Ike appears to have urged two of his top aides—his chief of staff, Adams, and chair of the CEA, Burns—to study the possibility of highway legislation.[28] These are the most definitive instructions for pursuing highway expansion the president appears to have given since his inauguration, but if the activity his instructions precipitated is any indication, he was perceived by his advisors to be still very much in the "study" and "exploration" stage of planning. Indeed, "several top officials were busy developing plans. But each chose to interpret Eisenhower's instructions differently. Old fissures between administrators appeared quickly, then, as each produced different proposals to finance and control construction and apportion funds."[29] This particular outcome is unsurprising, given that Eisenhower had made few of his priorities for roadbuilding clear. Accordingly, in the months following the April 12 White House meeting, during the summer of 1954, Burns and Adams chose to investigate highway expansion in very different ways, and to propose radically different legislation.

Burns largely delegated Eisenhower's assignment to Bragdon, who decided to move the ball forward quite aggressively. Sensing the president's ambivalence during the April 12 meeting, Bragdon later in the same day spoke with two officials who would be instrumental to any future highway program. He telephoned Walker Buckner to discuss "his memorandum (given me by Dr. Hauge) on subject of self-liquidating projects," and then made arrangements to see Buckner in New York within a few days. Bragdon also had lunch with Du Pont.[30] We have seen that Eisenhower had sent Burns a confidential memorandum on February 2, 1954, asking the CEA to study the possibility of implementing public works programs to mitigate unemployment during a possible depression. As part of Burns's team, Bragdon would have received the president's message and would have therefore been aware that Ike was interested in using highway projects as emergency economic measures.

As he had done in speaking with Robert Murray a few days before, Bragdon did not raise the subject of Buckner's report (which Du Pont would have read), but instead merely floated the idea of "road work as a means of providing employment in a recession." In response, Du Pont quickly made it clear that by using existing congressionally authorized funds, they would "not be able to do very much acceleration"—meaning little would change in terms of the BPR's ability to create additional road-building jobs in case of economic emergency without new legislation. As the conversation continued, Du Pont described "what he thought was a radical, but nevertheless perfectly feasible solution to the entire highway problem." Du Pont urged Bragdon no longer to see highway expansion merely as means to combatting unemployment and deflation, but as a project worthy of pursuing in its own right for the sake of the national interest. Specifically, Du Pont argued that expansion of the federal highway system should be a national priority (1) on account of national defense; (2) because of "product distribution," that is, growing the economy in the long run by putting the vast country's many markets in contact with each other more efficiently; and (3) because federal highways are the "central core of the entire highway systems," that is, that state, county, and municipal routes are subordinate to federal ones.[31]

Du Pont clearly favored overhauling the Federal-Aid program instead of expanding it incrementally, as his predecessor MacDonald had preferred. He was also in favor of expanding highways for reasons other than mitigating the effects of an economic downturn, another source of ambivalence for Eisenhower. Perhaps most crucial of all, he suggested to Bragdon that the best way to finance highway construction would be through bonds issued by a "national highway authority" and paid by revenue from one cent of the federal gas tax.[32] Precisely what Du Pont had in mind for a national highway authority he did not elaborate, but the general thrust of his plan would seem to have been that the federal government should borrow the money, because adopting a "pay as you go" approach would take too long.

In the weeks following his meetings with Buckner, Du Pont, and Murray, Bragdon wasted no time generating a highway bill of his own, one that clearly drew inspiration from Du Pont's more centrally planned vision. On April 16, 1954, Bragdon outlined a brief, one-page "National Defense Highway Bill" with eight priorities.[33] The overall thrust of the outline is that the new highway system should be headed by a single director, housed within the existing BPR, with broad authority to spend funds and select routes. Bragdon continued to work on the outline in subsequent days, meeting Buckner for lunch in New York on April 19, and sending him a full draft of a proposed bill on April 21, requesting feedback.[34] In his cover letter to Buckner, Bragdon notes that he wrote the draft "along the lines of our discussion"—presumably a reference to their lunch meeting three days before. Bragdon adds that he "has no pride of authorship" of the draft, which is "really a collection of provisions which technicians would have to put into shape." Bragdon makes a point to ask Buckner to "please examine especially the paragraphs having to do with financing," an unsurprising request, given that Bragdon's original outline included no details to this effect. Accordingly, Bragdon's bill draft is for the most part an elaboration of his April 16 outline. Bragdon elaborates to some degree the relationship he envisions between the states and the federal government. Rose notes that for Bragdon, "highway construction was a national obligation," "not something to be divided and left to local governments."[35] The Bragdon plan specifies that although the director of the highway program "shall confer with the State Governor and their principal highway officials" about "routing, financing, and construction," at the end of the day, it is the director who will make the "final decision."[36]

As for financing, Bragdon's draft largely builds upon Buckner's original report to Eisenhower from early 1953. Bragdon suggests that "financing of the national highway system will be by States or State agencies with authority to issue bonds, such securities to be guaranteed by the Federal Government both as to principal and interest."[37] However, unlike the Buckner proposal, which seemed to prevaricate about whether bonds issued for highway construction would count against the national debt, paragraph 9 of Bragdon's draft states quite plainly that the director of the highway system will be "authorized to guarantee such issues [of bonds] with the credit of the U.S.," thereby clarifying that the highway bill should acknowledge that the federal government would, in fact, be incurring a debt in order to finance highway expansion. Bragdon appears to have recognized that the only way to expand highways rapidly instead of incrementally would be to increase the amount of money authorized by the Federal-Aid program. Doubtless aware of Eisenhower's commitment to avoid increasing the country's indebtedness, Bragdon nevertheless makes the hard choice that the president was, at this point, unwilling to make, and recommends borrowing as the best means to advance the project.

While Bragdon was pushing his plan forward with the help of Buckner and Commissioner Du Pont, Adams was taking a more hands-off approach. Ten days after the White House meeting that launched this new phase of study, Adams met with legendary New York highway builders Robert Moses and Bertram D. Tallamy on April 21, 1954. Moses had dominated highway building in New York City since the Depression and had developed a national reputation. Tallamy would go on to be named by Eisenhower as federal highway administrator under the 1956 Highway Act. The priorities of the plan Adams recommended to Moses and Tallamy were "more consonant with American road-building traditions."[38] Likely as a consequence of his own experience as governor of New Hampshire, in which capacity he would have balanced the need for federal aid with traditional state prerogatives, Adams was significantly more sensitive than was Bragdon to the felt needs of state governments in the area of roadbuilding. Indeed, "the Federal and state cooperation that Thomas MacDonald had established in the Bureau of Public Roads . . . had worked well when [Adams] was governor of New Hampshire, and if the Federal government increased funding, it would work even better."[39]

On May 4, 1954, Tallamy and Moses sent Adams a cover letter and an outline of a bill for highway expansion. Their plan would create a new federal highway authority tasked with raising an additional $15 billion in highway funds while basically leaving state and local roadbuilding capacities in place.[40] For their parts, Moses and Tallamy were upfront that they "doubt[ed] whether any definitive, carefully worded act satisfactory to Congress [could] be drafted at this time,"[41] thereby casting doubt on the president's hopes that highway legislation might be used to bolster the GOP's chances of holding Congress in the 1954 midterms. At the same time, the authors also observed that they believed that "with Presidential sponsorship an agreement on objectives and machinery might be reached promptly, to be followed by submission of a more detailed plan and further legislation later in the year." The authors concluded that "the way will be paved for action in 1955."

Crucially, the Moses-Tallamy plan estimated that the federal contribution to the proposed highway program would be roughly "fifteen billion dollars," but "an estimated grand total of fifty billion dollars" would be needed "to establish a safe, modern, and adequate state and local highway system." The number of $50 billion was especially impressive to Eisenhower, who on May 11 wrote to Adams: "Where do we stand on our 'dramatic' plan to get 50 billion dollars with of self-liquidating highways under construction?"[42] Aware that the two factions headed by Adams and Bragdon were at loggerheads, and that consensus on a concrete plan was still a long way off, Ike was trying to make sure that the project did not stall out altogether. But he was also paying the price for having assigned two inimical personalities an open-ended task, without indicating a time frame for completion or meeting with the whole group on a regular basis to collaborate and assess the project's status. As a consequence, Bragdon and Adams had pursued their studies separately in consultation with individuals with radically diverging interests.

For these reasons, by midsummer 1954, Bragdon and Adams were trying to find ways to outflank each other to obtain the president's approval for their preferred approach. Yet neither had reason to believe that his respective plan would be obviously superior to the other's, that it would be sufficiently attractive to Eisenhower, or that it would stand a chance in Congress. Hence, on May 11, the same day Eisenhower wrote to him asking about the status of his highway plan, Adams wrote to Budget Director Dodge observing that some "power plays" would be needed to secure presidential approval of the Moses–Tallamy plan.[43] His efforts failed, however, and on May 24, Bragdon sent a critique of Moses–Tallamy to Burns.[44] Bragdon's two main points of contention concerned the continued role that the BPR would play in highway expansion under the Moses–Tallamy plan and the authority it would delegate to state and local roadbuilders.[45] Bragdon was insistent that existing federal roadbuilding bureaucracy and local authorities were a hindrance to meaningful progress in highway expansion. For his part, Bragdon continued to review drafts of his own plan throughout May and into June, but he appears never to have submitted a complete draft for Eisenhower's approval.[46]

Deadlock

As of June 1954, more than a year and a half after he commissioned Walker Buckner to draft a highway plan, Eisenhower's administration had done little to advance highway expansion besides unearthing the same basic conflicts that had bedeviled previous presidents who had attempted to pursue the same goal. Part of the problem seems to have been that Eisenhower simply lacked a sense of clear purpose. He knew he wanted to pursue the abstract goal of highway expansion, but he did not understand how to translate that goal into concrete steps toward meaningful action. We have seen how Ike vacillated from the very outset of his presidency about two basic aspects of highway expansion. The first concerned timing. When and in what order should study of highway expansion materialize into action? Should the administration set deadlines for itself? Was the project urgent or would it benefit from prolonged study? The second aspect concerned Congress. During this period, Eisenhower was consistently tentative regarding whether, or the extent to which, he wanted the legislature to be involved with highway expansion.

These aspects are clearly interrelated. Early on, Eisenhower had suggested that he wanted to reallocate funds previously appropriated by Congress for roadbuilding projects in order to stimulate the economy and avert a recession after the Korean War. In turn, Eisenhower believed action in this area would help the Republicans retain their majorities in Congress during the 1954 elections. This was certainly the impression he gave at his February 5, 1954, cabinet meeting, where Treasury Secretary Humphrey, building on Eisenhower's remarks, made a point of emphasizing the importance of holding Congress. Seen from this standpoint, highway expansion would have been deployed chiefly as a means to holding the Congress in the case of significant economic trouble. But if this was in fact the principal rationale for new roadbuilding projects, then it also would have required fast action—sometime well before the summer of 1954—in order to make that outcome more likely. By prolonging study of the issue, and failing to settle on a specific plan, Eisenhower made it increasingly difficult to rationalize roadbuilding as a means to hold Congress. The longer he waited, the less likely a roadbuilding project would affect the outcome of the midterms. Further, once it become clear that the economy would not suffer a significant postwar recession, using roadbuilding as a make-work project to avert economic downturn no longer seemed relevant. For his part, even after it was clear he had averted a recession in early 1954, Eisenhower never suggested he was no longer committed to highway expansion. How, then, did he propose to rationalize highway expansion, once it became clear that any significant highway expansion would happen too late to affect the outcome of the 1954 midterm elections, indeed, that it would likely happen *after* the elections?

Originally, Eisenhower justified pursuing highway expansion without Congress on the grounds that urgent action in the area of roadbuilding would be required to head off a negative reaction in the 1954 midterms to an economic downturn, and that Congress would take too long to act in time to make a difference. But once the economy improved, and the sense of urgency disappeared as a result, the need to act unilaterally without congressional authorization also diminished. Urgently deploying make-work roadbuilding programs before the 1954 midterms in the absence of mass unemployment would serve no obvious purpose; it would also discredit Eisenhower's argument that the New Deal coalition had been too willing to spend government money on make-work for no good reason, thereby contributing to waste and indebtedness. For this reason, if Eisenhower was still serious about truly meaningful highway expansion even after the 1953 recession had passed, his only good option was to work through Congress to obtain truly transformative highway legislation, as opposed to pursuing piecemeal roadbuilding projects unilaterally. And as it would soon become clear, Eisenhower would need Republican majorities in Congress if he was going to pass his preferred highway plan as opposed to a Democratic alternative.

It is at this point that the variables of time and Congress converged as a single problem that was not within Eisenhower's power to solve. For by mid-1954, it was far from clear whether the Republicans would hold their slim majorities in either house of Congress. Further, as the state of the three highway proposals on the table as of June 1954 makes clear, passing a major highway bill before the end of the 1954 congressional session—while the GOP could still depend on its majorities—was simply a nonstarter. Indeed, the Moses-Tallamy plan stated explicitly that feasible legislation could not be generated until 1955, at the earliest. And by then, it was anyone's guess which party would control Congress.

Before proceeding to the next stage of Eisenhower's broader effort, it is worth reflecting briefly on the alternative decisions that would seem to have been open to the president before summer 1954. The first concerns Ike's relationship with Congress, and specifically congressional Republicans, during the early months of his first term. Eisenhower did not make highway expansion one of his legislative priorities during his early meetings with Senator Robert A. Taft (R-Ohio) and other GOP leaders in Congress—even though he had already commissioned Buckner to draw up a plan for highway legislation before his first term began. One obvious question this decision raises is why Eisenhower chose not to consult with the congressional leadership during these early stages, instead confining research and development within his administration. As his early legislative meetings with the congressional GOP confirm, Eisenhower was clearly willing to let congressional leaders take the reins on other major legislative issues. Why not highways, too?

The most plausible explanation concerns Eisenhower's relationship (or lack thereof) with the two parties. Eisenhower had tenuous connections with GOP leadership, having decided to formally affiliate himself with the Republican Party only shortly before deciding to run for president in the first place. On this score, the president consistently expressed frustration with members of the GOP, and especially with congressional Republicans on the party's right wing, in his private correspondences and diary entries. On several occasions he even stated privately his desire to form a third, "middle of the road" party made up of moderate Republicans and Democrats. His closest personal connections were not with elected officials and politicians, but with members of the armed forces whom he had known professionally, and with business leaders whom he had come to know and trust during his period of elite socialization following the war.

Eisenhower's reluctance to work through traditional congressional channels during the early stages of highway legislation development was therefore likely a consequence of his lacking a meaningful network of political connections in either party. Indeed, during the initial stage of development, the figures who played the most significant roles in helping Eisenhower create highway legislation—Walker Buckner (Wall Street), J. S. Bragdon (army officer), Gabriel Hauge (banker), Francis du Pont (state highway official), George Humphrey (businessman), and Lucius Clay (army officer and businessman)—were all nonpoliticians. The one exception, Sherman Adams, had made a relatively late entry to politics after a career in lumber and banking.[47]

Because Eisenhower had yet to involve Congress in his plans for highway expansion by the summer of 1954, it seemed less likely than ever that he would be able to assemble majorities in both houses of Congress to pass his preferred plan before the 1954 midterms. Eisenhower clearly wanted to shape the process by which highway legislation was formed, rather than allow congressional Republicans—with whom he frequently disagreed and whose different wings had a difficult enough time working together—either produce a bill that he could not support or, what seems the more likely outcome, fail to produce a bill altogether as a consequence of the very contradictions that had bedeviled his own administration. As an added difficulty, Eisenhower was clearly less than confident both in his own grasp of the tradeoffs that a significant highway bill would entail and in his ability to manage the unwieldy coalition that would be needed to see such a bill through to the end.

CHAPTER 3

The Clay Committee and the Development of Eisenhower's Highway Program, 1954–1955

Lucius Clay represents the fiery type of fellow that you see in old-fashioned movies.
—Robert A. Lovett

From the very outset, Eisenhower's decision to invest new energy in highway reform ran into trouble. He had planned to deliver a speech to the Annual Conference of Governors in Lake George, New York, on July 12, 1954, announcing his administration's commitment to a dramatic plan for highway expansion. But because of a last-minute death in his wife's family, he had to either postpone the speech or delegate the task of reading his text to a member of his administration. He took the latter path and chose Vice President Richard Nixon for the job.[1] Delivered by Nixon, the address announced that the Eisenhower administration would pursue a "50 billion dollar highway program" over the next ten years.[2] In the weeks following Nixon's speech, the president appointed two new committees to study highway expansion and to create legislation that might be sent to Congress around the time of the State of the Union Address in January 1955. But in November 1954, Eisenhower lost his Republican majorities in the House and Senate, forcing him and his committees to interact with new Democratic majorities.

In many ways, the subject of this chapter—Eisenhower's decisions to support highway legislation during the summer and fall of 1954—stands as the most complicated puzzle we will encounter. From both deliberative and strategic standpoints, Ike's choices relating to highway policy during this period often seem incoherent and impulsive. The characteristic caution and thoughtfulness that marked his initial forays into the subject appear to have been replaced with impatience and an overall lack of foresight. Indeed, as we will see in chapter 5, it was congressional Democrats who salvaged interstate highway expansion after Eisenhower and his administration so clearly mismanaged it.

"$50 Billion in Self-Liquidating Highways"

This change in behavior is manifest in Eisenhower's decision to give the July 12 speech, and in the content of the speech itself. As of June 1954, the members of Eisenhower's administration who had been tasked with studying highway expansion were at loggerheads, and the president was clearly unwilling to throw his weight behind one of the three contradicting plans that his advisors had produced. Yet because he was still committed to highway expansion as a general principle, he did not want to lose whatever momentum he had managed to generate toward that end. So Ike decided to shift tactics. Whereas previously he had pursued highway research within the White House and the Executive Office, making only vague and cagey statements about highway reform before the public, at the Governors' Conference he would announce for the first time a dramatic new plan before a widely publicized audience.

Eisenhower's speech is remarkable in two respects. The first is the sheer magnitude of the number that the president proposes spending: $50 billion in 1954 dollars is equivalent to $527 billion in 2022 dollars.[3] Eisenhower was suggesting the government should increase its spending on highways from roughly $500 million a year—the number determined in the 1954 Federal-Aid Act—to $5 billion a year under the new proposal: a tenfold increase. To help further contextualize that number, the proposed annual budget for fiscal year 1955 was $62.7 billion.[4] Eisenhower was proposing to spend over ten years almost the equivalent of an entire year's federal budget on highways alone.

More significant than the expense itself was that, at the time of Eisenhower's speech, there simply was no plan for where the money would come from or how it would be spent. The figure was arbitrary. As of July 1954, the president's advisors had produced three competing plans for highway expansion, and none of these were near being ready for submission to Congress. The number of $50 billion had been included in the Moses-Tallamy plan, but its authors had also made a point of insisting that an actual highway bill would not be ready until at least 1955, and Eisenhower had in no way indicated that he planned to adopt that plan in particular. As might be expected, the proposal that Eisenhower actually describes in his July 12 speech is no more developed than his previous descriptions of highway expansion from earlier in his term. He speaks of "enterprises" that are "self-liquidating," but without describing in any detail the mode by which revenue would be raised or how expenditures would be apportioned,[5] calling for "a financing proposal based on self-liquidation of each project, wherever that is possible, through tolls or the assured increase of gas tax revenue, or on Federal help where the national interest demands it."[6] He calls for a "middle ground" between "local initiative" and federal supervision, but without clarifying the hard choices that will have to be made in drawing lines of authority.[7] The only significant differences between this speech and previous public statements that Eisenhower had made regarding highway expansion were that he had never previously assigned a dollar value to the project, and he had never previously claimed to have a plan for how to spend those dollars.

Why would Eisenhower propose $50 billion in highway financing and construction if he did not have a more specific proposal to substantiate and justify that number?[8] One way of interpreting the July 12 speech is that the president was merely sketching the broad outlines of a project on whose principles he wished the Congress to deliberate. A speech of that kind would have been entirely consistent with relations between the president and Congress going back to the nineteenth century.[9] That Eisenhower was asking Congress to deliberate on and elaborate the details of a set of core policy priorities is belied by the text of the speech itself, however. The president nowhere actually calls upon Congress to take up the issue, instead speaking as though the number of $50 billion had already been settled on by his administration. Indeed, by presenting his first dramatic call for highway expansion at the Governors' Conference, Eisenhower appeared to be signaling that the views of the state governments were just as important for highway expansion as the views of Congress, if not more so. This was an odd signal to send, given that in the end Eisenhower was advocating for expanded *federal* action in the area of roadbuilding, and that it would therefore be Congress, and not the state governors, who would have to authorize any proposed expansion of federal highway capacities.

For their parts, the governors seem to have taken the president's announcement seriously, and to have regarded themselves as his primary audience. Several days later, near the end of the Lake George conference, they passed a resolution establishing a committee to study highway expansion. This committee would receive reports from all forty-eight state governments concerning the condition of their highway programs; in turn, the committee was supposed to synthesize these reports into a recommendation to be sent to the president by November 1, 1954.[10]

Reporters were quick to seize on the element of Eisenhower's highway speech that was least developed and that had bedeviled previous attempts at highway expansion: funding. Two days after Nixon delivered the speech, during a July 14 press conference, Eisenhower was asked by Glen Thompson of the *Cincinnati Enquirer* how "$50 billion in highway building should be financed."[11] Unsurprisingly, given his manner of addressing this question so far, Eisenhower immediately disclaimed having any particular financing mode in mind: "Well, I don't think there is any one way." Recognizing that this response was likely to seem odd given his apparent commitment to the figure of $50 billion, the president immediately conceded that "all [he had] made was a proposition." Indeed, "we are *at least* $50 billion behind in our road networks" (my emphasis). Whereas the reporter clearly interpreted the president's speech as an announcement of a plan, one that would require a specific amount of funding, here Eisenhower tries to clarify that the specific number he stated was merely a goal, and that there was no plan in place whose design actually required that amount of funding. A few moments later, the president reiterates, "I have no definite plan," and adds that "we have been studying it for a year," before concluding with two formulations that by now should be familiar: "By and large, [the new highway plan] should be local and, I would say, exploit the self-liquidating idea as far as possible."

A Tale of Two Committees, Part II

The clearest indication Eisenhower gave that he did not intend to seek congressional involvement at this stage of development came in the weeks immediately following the July 12 speech. Eisenhower asked Sherman Adams to plan a path forward for highway legislation, and on July 22, 1954, Ike met with various members of his administration who had been involved in highway plans, including Adams and Bragdon. Adams presented the president with a two-page memorandum on the "status of the national highway program" outlining the steps he believed the administration should take next.[12] In his plan, Adams recommended creating two distinct committees to study highway expansion. An "Inter-Agency Committee" (IAC) would consist in members of relevant federal agencies, including the Bureau of Public Roads (BPR), Treasury, Defense, and the Budget Bureau. The job of this committee would be to "examine national highway needs, economic factors involved, and the development of plans—both for construction and financing—to satisfy the recommendations of the national program."[13]

A second committee, to be known as the "President's Advisory Committee" (PAC) would consider "recommendations of the Federal Government Inter-Agency Committee, the Governors' Conference, and Highway Users Conference, and other public and private recommendations dealing with the national highway plan." According to Adams's proposal, the PAC would synthesize these inputs into a plan that would be recommended to the president, who in turn would transmit legislation to Congress: "The recommendation of this Presidential Commission as approved by the president will be made a part of the Report to the Congress of the state of the Union in January 1955." Significantly, Adams charges the PAC with implementing "an aggressive campaign for the adoption of the program in the Congress" once the president has actually submitted his bill to the legislature. The plan does not involve the Congress in the actual development of highway legislation; it simply makes the PAC the president's chief lobbyist for its own bill in Congress.[14]

As for the composition of the PAC, Adams recommends that the president choose a chairman from the private sector to lead the group.

For this position, Adams suggests Roger Kyes, an executive at General Motors and former deputy secretary of defense under Secretary Charles Wilson.[15] The rest of the PAC would be composed of "not less than five nor more than nine members" with experience in "highway planning and administration," "toll road and freeway financing," and "administrative government at the local level."

At the July 22 meeting, Adams took some time to explain his memorandum, and his remarks were summarized by Bragdon.[16] Adams specifies that the members of the PAC should be "members of the public" (i.e., not government officials) and that the PAC would function as an "information-gathering commission." He also states that Commissioner Du Pont should chair the IAC. Adams concludes his remarks by reiterating that whoever leads the PAC would need to be involved in lobbying for the president's bill in Congress, and to that end he suggests meeting with congressional Republican leaders, including Speaker of the House Joseph Martin and Chairman of the House Committee on Public Works George Dondero, who would be "sponsors at the proper time." Eisenhower approved the plan and concluded the meeting by asking Adams for a brief memo before his call to Roger Kyes "tomorrow morning."[17]

Before turning to the events precipitated by Adams's proposal and Eisenhower's assent to that proposal, it is worth reflecting on what Eisenhower agreed to on July 22 and why he is likely to have agreed to it. The Adams memo appears in part to be a response to the stasis and logjam occasioned by the previous two groups Eisenhower had instructed to study highway reform (not counting Du Pont and the BPR, who had been conducting their own research alongside Bragdon and Adams). For his part, Adams was clearly frustrated working within existing government channels, and he appears to have been following the example of Eisenhower—who early on had enlisted private equity banker Walker Buckner—in turning to the private sector for a fresh perspective. For this reason, it is all the more striking that Adams chose to create a second committee consisting in interested government officials: the very people the PAC was designed to circumvent. Had not the stalemate within the administration during the spring of 1954 confirmed that clearer lines of authority needed to be drawn in order to actually produce a workable highway plan? Furthermore, even though it is clear Adams was trying to assign the two new committees their own responsibilities—he makes the point of saying that it will be the PAC that will actually draw up the proposal and lobby for it in Congress—it is also clear from the start that the ambiguous role of the IAC would lead to conflict. Unlike the PAC, the IAC consisted in government officials who had already affiliated themselves with specific visions of highway policy, who had deep roots in the roadbuilding tradition, and who were therefore unlikely to acquiesce in the plans of an ad hoc committee of private-sector elites. The rationale behind creating such a committee was tenable enough—they would contribute their knowledge and expertise to the PAC, who in turn would synthesize those insights into concrete legislation—but experience and common sense would seem to have suggested early on that members of the IAC, feeling sidelined in an area of policy they felt (not without some justification) belonged to them, were more likely to undermine the efforts of the PAC than they were to passively provide it with the information and counsel it needed.

From a strategic standpoint, Eisenhower's decision to authorize these two new committees is at the very least puzzling, but from a purely managerial standpoint, his rationale makes more sense. The same institutional incentives that would lead the IAC to resist and undermine the PAC would also lead them to resist the effort in possibly more damaging ways were Eisenhower to exclude them from the process of highway reform entirely. After all, it was going to be members of the federal government—and specifically, Eisenhower's own appointees, such as Du Pont, Humphrey, and Weeks—who would have to support and administer whatever plan the PAC created (assuming it passed Congress). Adams's pro forma inclusion of these officials in the process was clearly an effort to placate potential insurgents within the administration. Yet because they had been included as a concession to the federal bureaucracy—that is, for transparently managerial reasons, as opposed to genuinely functional ones—it was likely from the start that they would exist in an uneasy tension with the PAC, playing second fiddle to those whose vision and agenda the president clearly prioritized.

A second puzzling feature of Adams's plan is its proposed timeline. Adams indicates that the PAC's bill should be submitted to Congress through sympathetic Republican sponsors (such as George Dondero and

Joseph Martin) around the time of the president's 1955 State of the Union—that is to say, the first major address following the 1954 midterms. Clearly he had given up on the idea—previously floated by the president and by Secretary Humphrey—that new highway legislation could be used as a means to *win* the midterms. Now, it seemed, the midterms would have to be the means for winning highway legislation. Was Adams assuming that congressional Republicans would hold both of their majorities? If so, he seems to have anticipated either that the PAC's bill would attract enough bipartisan support to overcome any resistance by hardline conservatives or that the Republican majorities would be able and willing, if need be, to pass the administration's bill on a party-line vote.

Neither of these assumptions were safe. It is true that Eisenhower cherished hopes of a more bipartisan relationship with the Democratic Party, and that on certain occasions he had even had more luck working with congressional Democrats than with Republicans. Yet the idea that New Deal Democrats would be particularly receptive to a highway bill that they had played no role in designing—indeed, that had been cooked up by a team of business elites and then vetted by Republican state governors—is hard to fathom. Equally difficult to understand is Adams's apparent assumption that the GOP would hold the House and the Senate in the 1954 midterms and that the PAC's bill would therefore stand a chance in Congress.[18]

The president accepted Adams's plan and put him in charge of organizing both committees. The first major hurdle Adams had to clear was finding someone that fit the profile sketched in his plan to chair the PAC. Adams had suggested Kyes, and on Friday, July 23, Eisenhower phoned Kyes with the request.[19] Kyes took a day and a half to think about it, and replied by telegram at 8:35 P.M. Saturday politely declining Eisenhower's offer. Kyes's reasoning was that his presence as a private businessman on a committee recommending government action might be perceived as presenting a conflict of interest: "Major difficulty is that what might be considered selfish interest of corporation in such a program could prove detrimental to my effectiveness."[20] This concern appears not to have occurred to Adams or the president when they originally reviewed the plan on July 22, and it clearly did not dissuade them from attempting to recruit other businessmen once Kyes declined.

Accordingly, in the days following Kyes's telegram, members of the administration began considering other prominent business and corporate figures. Once news of Kyes's decision reached him, Adams asked Frank Bane, an economist and sociologist who held leadership positions in the Governors' Conference and the Council of State Governments, for additional suggestions.[21] Bane sent Adams a memo on July 26 with a list of prominent business and financial personnel, including Kyes (who had already declined), Chester Barnard of the Rockefeller Foundation, Robert Johnson (chairman of Johnson & Johnson), and James Palmer (president of Marshall Field & Co., a chain of department stores later acquired by Macy's).[22] On the same day, Gabriel Hauge wrote a floridly worded note to Adams recommending Kyes for the position: "My cogitations on a man to head the road committee produces nothing equal to Roger Kyes."[23] Clearly, Hauge had not yet received news of Kyes's decision.

Adams continued to solicit recommendations for men who were prominent in their respective fields of private industry. On July 27, Charles F. Willis Jr., an assistant chief of staff, sent Adams two memos on the subject of who should chair the PAC. On one, he recommends Stephen Bechtel—founder and president of the nationwide construction company, the Bechtel Corporation—observing that Vice President Nixon (previously a US representative and senator from California) knew the California businessman and was "very impressed by him."[24] In a second note to Adams, Willis—who, like Hauge, appears not to have been told about Kyes's decision—recommends against appointing Kyes.[25] Even though Willis's objection was by this time moot, his rationale is actually quite revealing as to Adams's broader goals regarding the PAC, goals that Adams had presumably expressed, or at least intimated, to Willis in the days following his July 22 meeting with Eisenhower. Specifically, Willis asserts that Kyes is "a very difficult man to get along with" and that "he considers himself above practical politics." Willis regards this behavior attribute as problematic because "there is a considerable amount of selling to do with the Governors of the various states to get them to go along with this program so they will not feel that their states' rights have been usurped." Willis does not "think that Mr. Kyes would have much patience with the diplomatic approach that this job would require." This statement suggests that Adams conceived of the role in question as, in part, a kind of liaison between the president and the state governors, who would have to be persuaded to endorse whatever plan the PAC eventually settled on. Such a perspective squares with Adams's commitment, expressed in his consultations with Moses and Tallamy, to preserving to the greatest extent possible state and local prerogative in the area of federal highway expansion. In contrast, the Bragdon/Burns wing of the administration had favored a more top-down approach. In accordance with the president's previous statements about states' rights and his decision to announce his $50 billion commitment at the 1954 Governors' Conference, Adams appears to have been looking for someone to chair the PAC who possessed the political adroitness to convince state officials to cooperate with the highway plan he envisioned.

Three days later, as of July 30, the president had yet to settle on someone to chair the PAC. He had asked Kyes and John Collyer, president of B. F. Goodrich (a tire manufacturer), and both had declined the request.[26] On July 30, Willis sent Adams a note suggesting several other business leaders to consider, including the presidents and CEOs of Scott Paper, Swift & Co. (a meat processing company) and Sears, Roebuck & Co.

Around this time, Adams received an additional proposal for highway expansion from several state highway officials who had been commissioned by Francis du Pont several months previous. Their report was similar to the plan Moses and Tallamy had submitted to Adams back in May, before the president's speech at the Governors' Conference:[27] "The thrust of their plan was to tighten relationships between Federal and State road engineers and augment everyone's revenue considerably." The plan also proposed repaying bonds with gas tax revenue.[28] The plan was circulated in late July and received harsh and immediate (and by this point, predictable) criticism from J. S. Bragdon, who in a series of memos to Arthur Burns from August 3 to August 6 enumerated reasons for rejecting this fourth plan.[29] As in previous exchanges, Bragdon faults the plan for raising insufficient funds, for leaving the states in charge instead of transferring authority to the federal government, for failing to replace the BPR with a new authority, and, in general, for not being ambitious and transformative enough.

Bragdon's exasperated memos from this point in the process are revealing as to the difficulties hard-wired into the process of developing highway legislation. On the one hand, Bragdon's tenacity and potent analytical skills enabled him to recognize and articulate contradictions in proposed expansion plans that other, more politically sensitive (and personally interested) actors involved in the process either wished to ignore or simply failed to see. For example, in his August 6 memorandum to Burns, Bragdon directly quotes language from the Du Pont proposal: "It would be the responsibility of the Bureau of Public Roads, also headed by the Commissioner of Public Roads, to establish the general design and construction policies for the Interstate System . . . and to insure that these are carried out by the states which would be directly responsible for the design and construction at present." Bragdon goes on to state bluntly: "This seems to be a contradiction in terms, i.e., the Commissioner of Public Roads is to 'establish the general design and construction policies' which are to be carried out 'by the states which would be directly responsible for the design and construction at present.' Which is it? Federal Government or states?" Bragdon concludes his critique: "It is still vague."[30] Anticipating the conflicts that were likely to unfold between state and federal highway officials as a consequence of unclear lines of authority like this one, Bragdon pressed the point that other officials, most notably Eisenhower himself, had been cautious about articulating: Expanding highways significantly beyond their current capacities would require making hard choices about the relative authority of the state and national governments, hard choices that would invariably alienate some part of the broader federal road-building coalition.

On the other hand, the very qualities that made Bragdon attentive to ambiguities and contradictions that other officials preferred not to confront head-on also tended to blind him to the legitimate concerns of competing voices within that same coalition. These qualities were in some respects a helpful antidote to Eisenhower's own inability to grasp contradictions and face tradeoffs squarely. Bragdon's standoff with Adams—another difficult man, albeit one more politically astute than Bragdon, who lacked Adams's capacity for building consensus—appears to have convinced Eisenhower that the internal contradictions of highway policy were more intractable than he had initially realized. Accordingly, Eisenhower's decision to appoint a new committee of nongovernment officials signaled his confidence in the ability of corporate and business elites to break through a governmental logjam. Whether that confidence was warranted we will consider in the final pages of this chapter.

Organizing the President's Advisory Committee

During late July and August, Adams and his staff continued to search for someone to chair the PAC. After several prominent business elites declined the president's offer, the position was finally accepted by Lucius Clay, a former general in the US Army, a close friend and confidant of Eisenhower's, and as of August 1954, the president of the Continental Can Company. On August 23, Adams phoned Clay asking him to come to Adams's office on the morning of August 30. Later that same day, Eisenhower's secretary Arthur Minnich sent White House Appointments Secretary Thomas Stephens a memorandum confirming that the president would meet with Clay, Governor Kohler of Wisconsin, and Gabriel Hauge on August 30 "to confer on the president's Highway Program."[31] The memo announces that Clay will chair the president's commission and that "the commission will probably have members from the Governors' Conference, that section of the public interested in highways, the administration and perhaps Congress." Clearly the president had not communicated to Minnich a clear idea of the people he wanted to work with Clay on the PAC. After the August 30 meeting, Clay sent the president a list of individuals he wanted to serve with him on the PAC.[32] The list included three businessmen—Stephen Bechtel of Bechtel Construction, William A. Roberts of Allis Chalmers, and Sloan Colt of Bankers Trust—in addition to one labor official: David Beck of the Teamsters Union. Clay anticipates the objection that none of the other possible interested parties—including state and local highway officials, members of the administration, and members of Congress—have direct representation on the PAC: "The viewpoints of municipalities, states, and other interested bodies will be obtained by direct and constant liaison," that is, they will only be consulted if Clay decides he wants their input.

Clay's rationale for this decision is that "the views of these special interests can better be obtained this way than by giving them direct representation on the committee."[33] Clay's rhetorical choices in this memo are revealing. He is clearly sensitive to the president's conviction that the most difficult roadblock impeding highway legislation is the presence of specifically *governmental* interest groups—what he dubs "special interests"—and that the key to progress is recruiting members of the business community who will be better positioned to devise a unilateral solution. That leaders of the banking, trucking, manufacturing, and construction sectors of the economy might themselves constitute "special interests," Clay chose not to mention to Eisenhower.

Nor did Eisenhower evidently regard the composition of his highway committee as problematic. Eisenhower authorized Clay's list, and on September 2, Clay wrote to Hauge notifying him that he had secured the acceptance of all four of the individuals he had previously proposed.[34] In turn, Hauge sent James Hagerty, Eisenhower's press secretary, a draft of a press release announcing the formation of the PAC. Revealingly, the original draft of the telegram stated that the committee would be "composed of five leading citizens with experience *and interests* in construction, finance, labor and agriculture."[35] In that draft, "interests" was crossed out with "background" inscribed above it. The telegram that was actually sent to Hagerty via Western Union reflected this revision.[36]

Changing "interests" to "background" reflected the administration's sensitivity to the allegation that Eisenhower's decisions had been unduly influenced by big business since the beginning of his term. In this particular instance, sensitivity was not unwarranted. Kyes had already turned Eisenhower down on the grounds that his involvement might raise suspicions of a conflict of interest. Now, in the case of the PAC, two of the advisory committee's members stood to profit directly from highway expansion. Dave Beck was in charge of the national trucking union, which depended on interstate routes perhaps more than any other industry. And Sloan Colt—like Walker Buckner, who had drawn up the original highway expansion plan back in late 1952—was an investment banker who would profit from the interest of highway construction bonds, were the committee to recommend and were Congress to authorize a plan that included bond financing. As business elites, every member of the committee stood to profit from highway expansion insofar as it opened up new markets to their industries and established more robust and interconnected supply chains.

Obtaining input and feedback from parts of the private sector who stand to profit from new government policies is by no means unusual in US politics, or for that matter, necessarily undesirable or illegitimate from the standpoint of the public interest. What is troubling about the arrangement of the PAC within the Eisenhower administration is that the president essentially farmed out the job of designing controversial and expensive new legislation to the private sector—and specifically to business elites who had never held public office and who stood to benefit from the legislation they drafted and approved. As Clay himself reported in an oral history years later, "Mr. Colt [the investment banker] was experienced in finance. We had to determine how we wanted to finance [the highway bill], and so his experience was invaluable."[37] To that end, the administration's own press release makes it clear that the PAC is fully in control of the process, and that input from the government officials and other members of the private sector would be taken into consideration at the sufferance of the PAC: "It is expected that the advisory committee will provide opportunity for interested individuals and groups to present their ideas and that it will also have the full assistance of the interdepartmental committee within the Executive Branch."[38] This hierarchy appears to have been a consequence of Eisenhower's decision to eschew any congressional involvement whatsoever in the actual drafting of highway legislation. By authorizing the PAC to hold hearings with public officials and members of the private sector, Eisenhower and Adams were clearly trying to preempt Congress. Holding hearings with administration-approved people and groups only, and then presenting Congress with a finished bill, would (they anticipated) enable them to circumvent a protracted congressional debate on the subject, one that would invariably require hearings and testimony from people and groups less than sympathetic with the administration's bill. Yet how they thought they could pull off such a maneuver even in a GOP-controlled Congress, let alone a Congress with new Democratic majorities, is difficult to fathom.

The 1954 Midterms

By the time Clay, the members of the PAC, and of the IAC began working on highway legislation in earnest, it was dawning on Eisenhower, his administration, and Republicans nationwide that the GOP stood a good chance of losing their majorities in Congress in the 1954 midterms. As the cases of Presidents Wilson, Hoover, and FDR were still in relatively recent memory, it was common knowledge that the president's party tended to lose rather than gain seats in Congress during midterm elections. There was also mounting contemporary evidence that this would happen too in 1954. As early as September 12, Republicans fared poorly in both federal and state elections in Maine, signaling possible difficulties for Republicans nationwide.[39] During October, prominent Republican officials, including former presidential candidate Thomas Dewey, complained to Eisenhower about his refusal to campaign for Republican candidates.[40] He initially refused to actively campaign for Republicans, but the president was eventually persuaded to enter the fray, and in the final days of the 1954 election undertook a nationwide speaking tour.

For all his talk of "the Middle Way," of forming an alliance with Democrats, and of reforming the Republican Party into a new, "progressive" political organization, Eisenhower was bewildered by the US Constitution's separation of powers system and believed that productive relations between Congress and the president were impossible unless the same party controlled both branches of government.[41] At a speech delivered at the Hollywood Bowl on September 23, 1954, kicking off his nationwide campaign for congressional Republicans, the president contended that "when, unfortunately, the Congress is controlled by one political party and the executive branch by the other, politics in Washington has a field day. The conduct of Government tends, under these conditions, to deteriorate into an endless round of contests for political advantage—an endless round of political maneuverings, of stagnation and inaction—of half measures or no measures at all."[42] More pointedly, Eisenhower at one point alleged that "a Democratic-controlled House and Senate would mean the return of divided government, the end of progress, and the start of 'a cold war of partisan politics.'" According to Hardeman and Bacon, this jab "was too tempting for [House Minority

Leader] Rayburn and [Senate Minority Leader] Johnson to ignore. They fired back a stinging telegram, reminding the president of past Democratic help and advising that any future 'cold war' would be of his making, not theirs."[43]

Eisenhower's remarks here were bizarre indeed, given his notorious difficulties with congressional Republicans and his relatively collegial working relationship with Minority Leader Lyndon Johnson and congressional Democrats—a fact Adams makes a point of emphasizing in his recollections of the 1954 midterms: Eisenhower "rarely received the unified and solid backing of his own party in the Senate and the House when he needed it most in 1953 and 1954 . . . a good many of the members of the [Republican] National Committee were either lukewarm or openly hostile to the president."[44]

Why Eisenhower refused to campaign for congressional Republicans until the very last second notwithstanding this conviction is itself a puzzle that deserves sustained treatment.[45] For present purposes, the most glaring contradiction in Ike's strategy is that in July 1954 he agreed to Adams's proposal before the results of the midterms had been determined; yet Adams's proposal did not propose submitting a highway bill to Congress until after the midterms. Given that Eisenhower felt he needed majorities in Congress in order to pass major pieces of legislation (such as, presumably, a massive highway bill), why would he have committed himself to a highway plan—one that was likely to be controversial, given the history of highway legislation in the United States—knowing that his party stood a good chance of losing their congressional majorities?

One possible explanation of Eisenhower's seemingly incoherent decision is that during the early stages of the PAC, when the White House was actually vetting potential members, the president's attention was being eaten up by international crises, including the Formosa standoff. On September 3, 1954—the very day Hauge wrote to Hagerty announcing who the members of the PAC would be—the People's Republic of China began shelling Quemoy, an island between mainland China and Taiwan (then called Formosa) held by the Chinese Nationalists.[46] Two US servicemen were killed, and the standoff that ensued between both sides of the Chinese civil war—and by extension, between the United States and communist forces allied with the People's Republic—threated to devolve into all-out war, with members of Eisenhower's own administration recommending the use of nuclear weapons. It is possible that Eisenhower was simply too distracted by these events, and other international conflicts, including the French war in Indochina, to devote sufficient time to the tactics of highway expansion.

Yet Eisenhower had agreed to Adams's plan for creating two separate committees in July 1954—well before the outset of the Formosa standoff. For this reason, it seems more probable that during the summer and fall of 1954, Eisenhower had simply allowed his impatience with highway expansion to hinder his ability to anticipate challenges that were likely to be posed by the 1954 midterms. After all, it appears that the Republicans (Eisenhower included) had not begun to seriously anticipate the possibility of Democratic victories until after Nixon had delivered Ike's July 12 speech to the governors. It is also likely that Eisenhower felt that his announcement of a $50 billion "plan" alone would increase his popularity with voters, by drumming up interest in an ambitious enterprise that had broad popular support.

To this end, Eisenhower was clearly attempting to use the promise of highway expansion, in addition to other legislative priorities, as a way to convince midterm voters to sustain or expand his majorities in Congress, majorities he would need in order to pass whatever legislation his administration produced following the midterms. For example, at his Hollywood Bowl speech, Eisenhower stated that "the next Congress" will have to consider "important legislation," including "a tremendous new highway program."[47] As we might expect given his previous statements about the need for unified party control of government, Eisenhower goes on to state that "for a political party in our Nation to be held clearly accountable to the people for its political philosophy and programs to guide the course of our Government, it is essential that that party control both the executive and the legislative branches of the Government. This is what all of you worked for in 1952." "These are the reasons," he concludes, "why the completion of your great program requires the election of a Republican-led Congress."[48]

A final consideration worth reflecting on is that there appears to have been some confusion as to what kinds of officials would actually constitute the PAC. Would they be government officials, roadbuilders and engineers, or members of the private sector? For his part, Clay recruited exclusively from the latter group, and Eisenhower was disinclined to interfere with Clay's decisions. After all, the PAC was an attempt to break through the stalemate that had hitherto marked all efforts at significant highway reform. Clay was the man Eisenhower settled on to overcome the routine negotiations and stalemates characteristic of highway coalition building, and if Clay felt he would be best served in his efforts by a team of businessmen, Eisenhower, whose affinity for private-sector solutions was a hallmark of his presidency, was far from likely to insist that Clay supplement his team with government bureaucrats. Yet as a consequence of this decision—which was made before Eisenhower had begun to seriously contemplate the possibility of Republican losses in the 1954 midterms—the president was stuck with a PAC whose composition was designed to alienate Democrats at the very same time that the Democrats' prospects for retaking Congress were improving. Eisenhower had organized the PAC to break through a logjam, and yet the very design of that committee made it incompatible with a Democratic Congress.

The Clay Committee

On November 2, 1954, the Democrats retook both houses of Congress, with slim majorities of two in the Senate and eight in the House of Representatives. As of November 2, both the PAC and the IAC had been working on their respective highway bills for roughly two months, and most if not all of the tensions and contradictions that had bedeviled the Adams and Bragdon study groups during the summer of 1954 had begun to set in there, too. Rose puts it best: "Within government circles, old conflicts resumed. Points of debate were roughly what they had been prior to Eisenhower's reorganization of the search committees [in July 1954]. Indeed, it was as if the president had never intervened."[49]

There were two particularly sensitive points of conflict. Because it was composed of government individuals who had previously been on opposite sides of the highway debate during 1953 and early 1954, the IAC "offered only a fresh forum into which the government men extended their deadlock."⁵⁰ Du Pont, Bragdon, and Moses–Tallamy (the last represented by Adams) had each advocated contradicting plans before Eisenhower decided to reshuffle the highway project. By placing Bragdon and Du Pont on the same committee during the reshuffle, however, the president simply channeled the debate he had wanted to resolve in a different direction. Du Pont had asked several state highway officials, including Tallamy, to draw up a highway proposal shortly after the July 22 meeting with the president.⁵¹ In turn, Bragdon had immediately rejected that proposal on the same grounds that he had objected to the proposal that had been put forward by Moses and Tallamy at the request of Adams in July. As a result, it is unsurprising that when the IAC met formally on September 9, a few days after the Clay Committee had been formally approved by the president, Bragdon objected when Du Pont submitted the new road expert plan for the PAC's approval.⁵² As before, his chief complaint was that the plan was insufficiently forward-looking, and that it left too much authority in the hands of state officials when national planning and financing were clearly imperative.⁵³

For what it is worth, that these differing perspectives continued to emerge even after Eisenhower's reorganization of the committees is unsurprising given the backgrounds of the two committee members who had the strongest opinions about the path forward. Because Du Pont was viewing the problem from the standpoint of road maintenance and traffic adequacy, his primary concern was with building roads that could meet contemporary and future traffic needs; he did not seem to conceive of federal highways and traffic patterns as themselves instrumental to any additional, more aspirational objectives. In contrast, Bragdon was a relative outsider to the roadbuilding community and was consequently dismissive of their concerns, which he regarded as excessively narrow and technical. In Rose's assessment, "Bragdon and members of his small group defined road policy as part of grander plans for economic improvement and social control . . . [Bragdon] anticipated greatly increased employment opportunities, especially in the automobile industry, and acceleration of economic growth along new expressways."⁵⁴ Clearly, Eisenhower's own limited utterances regarding the need for dramatic highway expansion were themselves reflections of these competing commitments, which he had been exposed to in the course of consulting the different members of his highway study group during 1953 and the first half of 1954. By the same token, Bragdon and Du Pont were each emphasizing different aspects of the general vision Eisenhower had attempted to articulate during the preceding months. Whatever plan the president eventually settled on would require significant tradeoffs. Du Pont's approach would seem crabbed and insufficiently ambitious from a more nationalizing and forward-looking viewpoint, whereas Du Pont would see Bragdon's plan as wasteful and excessively provocative toward the traditional locus of roadbuilding authority: counties and states.

Bragdon, Du Pont, and the other members of the IAC would have been well advised to save their energy disputing with each other over the highway plan the administration should endorse. As soon as he started work, it become clear that Clay was all but indifferent to the work of the IAC and that he was happy to exploit the ambiguous relationship between his committee and the IAC that had been established by Adams's plan.[55] Given Clay's personality, this outcome is unsurprising. A different, more politically astute chair of the PAC might have anticipated the IAC's eagerness to become—or rather, remain—involved in the process of developing a highway bill, and found ways to assuage their jealousy while ultimately minimizing their input. For his part, Clay did not possess the faculties to pursue such a strategy—or if he did, he refused to deploy them. "Though he had helped Eisenhower choose his cabinet in 1952," writes Lewis, "and though the president-elect had offered him a position in that cabinet, Clay would have nothing of the political life."[56] Lucius Clay was a descendent of Henry Clay, known in his day as "The Great Compromiser" for his roles in negotiating significant and controversial legislation during the antebellum period. For his part, Lucius Clay was known by some as "The Great Un-Compromiser" for his renowned intractability.[57] Eisenhower had been close enough with Clay in the preceding decades to understand the man's character and anticipate his inability to work cooperatively, let alone productively, with the bureaucrats and entrenched interests of the IAC.[58] As in the case of Bragdon, who appears to have shared significant personality traits with Clay, Eisenhower was clearly trying to use Clay's uncompromising and apolitical disposition to his advantage, as a means of circumventing the conflicting interests and institutional path-dependencies that had stymied previous attempts at highway reform.

Of course, the practical consequence of his decision to appoint Clay as head of the PAC was that Clay simply ignored the IAC's recommendations.[59] This immediately became a problem, because "by virtue of the president's instructions, or so they liked to think, Interagency members assumed a right to prior examination of Clay's proposals."[60] Key here is "so they liked to think"; unfortunately for the members of the IAC, there was no oversight built into Adams's original plan for organizing the two committees. This feature was likely by design: from the perspective of anti–New Deal Republicans, such as Eisenhower and Adams, additional procedures and red tape would have defeated the very purpose of appointing nongovernment officials to design the legislation in the first place. Consequently, the IAC had no way of forcing the PAC to comply with its orders besides threatening to withhold their endorsements of whatever plan Clay eventually settled on, which they did.[61]

By stonewalling the IAC, which included interested officials, such as the commissioner of the BPR and the secretaries of commerce and treasury, Clay had effectively called the federal bureaucracy's bluff. That Eisenhower had neither integrated these competing groups nor given the IAC a more prominent role in developing highway legislation signaled to Clay that the IAC had been formed in the first place less as a way to ensure their input than as a concession to their sense of institutional purpose. For this reason, he felt he could ignore them with relative impunity.

The input Clay did solicit from parties other than himself and the four members of the PAC came from interested actors in the private sector during hearings on October 7 and 8. Unsurprisingly, these hearings revealed the same lack of consensus about federal roadbuilding, particularly financing, that had stymied highway expansion for over a generation.[62] As Lewis notes, "everyone agreed that the United States needed better roads and an interstate highway system, but the lobbyists disagreed as sharply as the president's advisers about how to achieve their goal."[63] This disagreement manifested itself materially in the "web" of groups interested in highway policy, including highway, automobile, trucking, and petroleum groups, many of which had been operating since the turn of the century. Accordingly, at the PAC's public hearings, "the spokesmen for each of the twenty-two lobbying groups invited to testify before the committee did little to clarify matters."[64] And once again, the question of how new highways would be funded took center stage: "'hearings which the [Clay] ... Committee held ... did not reveal any ... consensus with respect to ... finance.' What it came down to was that 'suggestions reflected ... the interests of the group which the speaker represented.'"[65] As had been the case during previous debates over highway policy, each of the private-sector groups that was to be materially affected by any significant changes to existing roadways advocated for changes that would benefit them directly and refused to pay for changes that would benefit other groups. In some cases, such as the trucking industry, interest groups even refused to pay for benefits that would help themselves: "The American Trucking Association lobbied hard for better roads and fewer taxes."[66] The explicit priority of each group was to obtain better roads for themselves—the American Automobile Association wanted more urban routes, representatives for small towns wanted rural routes, and truckers wanted both—by making someone else fund those routes.[67]

As a matter of coalition-building, the kind of collective action problem Clay and the members of the PAC were confronting in the fall of 1954 was by no means unusual. What is striking, though perhaps not surprising, about Clay's response to these interest groups is his decision to propose a funding mechanism that refused to even engage the difficult task of making users pay for new roadways through increased taxes. On December 1, 1954, Clay presented the broad outlines of his report at a meeting of the American Municipal Association (AMA) in Philadelphia.[68] In his presentation, Clay describes the constraints within which he and the members of the PAC were operating in attempting to create a workable highway plan. Under the heading, "Financing Without Tax Increase," Clay reiterates the administration's commitment to balancing the budget—one of Eisenhower's most emphatic campaign promises—and describes his search for a funding plan that would not require adding to the existing federal debt. Clay then states that the PAC was also instructed not to raise taxes to fund highway construction, because "the Federal government had embarked on a program of reduced, and not increased taxes."⁶⁹ Clay also makes clear that current gasoline tax rates being used to fund existing highway maintenance were entirely inadequate to building an interstate system that would meet the country's present and future demands: there was an "immediate and positive need" for $26 billion to finish highway expansion in the next ten years.⁷⁰ How to raise an enormous amount of federal cash in a short period of time without adding to the deficit or raising taxes was the challenge the PAC was facing.

Clay's proposed solution was to create a "Federal commission" that would "issue bonds in its own name," bonds it would repay over the course of thirty years with revenue from future gasoline and oil taxes.⁷¹ The most important feature of this plan was that by borrowing funds "in its own name" (and not in the name of the US Treasury), the new federal commission would, in theory at least, enable the federal government to avoid adding an additional deficit source to its budget. It would also enable the federal government to keep oil and gas taxes at the current rates, on the grounds that expanded future traffic and car ownership rates would allow the commission to repay its bonds without having to find additional sources of revenue.

The AMA voted to endorse the version of the PAC's plan that Clay had described, including his sketch of its financing mechanism. The basis of their endorsement was that "interstate highways are a capital asset which are properly paid for by capitalization because they lend themselves to long-term financing."⁷² However, the AMA makes no mention of the peculiar manner in which Clay was proposing to finance the new highways. Somehow, Clay believed, it was possible to borrow money that the federal government could use without the federal government having to count that money as its own debt. Would the federal government be obligated to repay creditors who purchased bonds? If not, would those creditors have any assurance that their bonds would be repaid whatsoever? What would be the legal status of the commission that issued those bonds if that commission was not borrowing under the authority of the US Treasury? What incentive would investors have if they had no guarantee that they would be able to recoup their principal in case of default, let alone the interest they were promised?

For his part, Clay publicly recognized the validity of these questions in his address to the AMA, even though it appears that he was not pressed about them. Clay certainly did not claim to have answers to these questions: "It is unusual to propose the borrowing of funds, not government funds but supported by government revenue for a ten-year period. I doubt if such a measure has been presented to the Congress."[73] Clay was right about this. And as chapter 4 will show, there were good reasons why no president before Eisenhower had ever asked Congress to do what Clay was proposing.

CHAPTER 4

Congress Resurgent
The Defeat of the Eisenhower Highway Bill in 1955

In a curious way, Eisenhower suffered from his strengths—particularly his self-confidence and his capacity for rational analysis. His certainty of the correctness of his own views could lead him to forget that what was self-evident to him might be obscure to others.
—Fred I. Greenstein

Sherman Adams's plan to create a Presidential Advisory Committee (PAC) to draw up highway legislation contained several directives that, even in expressing Eisenhower's hopes for a congenial and collaborative effort, could not easily be enforced in practice. Particularly, the plan anticipated that the PAC would willingly receive input from members of the federal bureaucracy and the Eisenhower administration. It also specified that the chair of the PAC would not only lead the effort to draft legislation but also lead a lobbying effort in Congress once the president had submitted his administration's bill. For his part, Lucius Clay ignored both of these directives. During the period in which he and the rest of the PAC were actually drafting their highway bill, he stonewalled John Bragdon and other members of the administration who had previously been involved in studying highway expansion,[1] turning instead to members of the public—and specifically, highway-related interest groups—who would be personally affected by any change in highway policy and who therefore had a personal stake in the outcome. He also incorporated feedback from the state governors, whose support Eisenhower had visibly attempted to enlist beginning with his July 12, 1954, speech (given by Vice President Nixon) at the Annual Governors' Conference.

Clay was also less than eager to engage members of Congress, either by soliciting their feedback during the drafting stage or by lobbying them once Eisenhower had formally sponsored his highway bill. This outcome is entirely unsurprising given Clay's personality and his reputation for political obtuseness. What is noteworthy is that, several months before, Eisenhower's assistant Charles Willis had advised against appointing Roger Kyes as chair of the PAC because he had anticipated that Kyes would be an ineffective advocate *for the very same reasons that Clay proved to be an ineffective advocate in practice*. According to Willis, Kyes was "a very difficult man to get along with," one who "consider[ed] himself above practical politics" and who would not "have much patience with the diplomatic approach that this job would require." Kyes's intractability would be a problem because there would be "a considerable amount of selling to do" in order to get the highway bill adopted.[2]

Willis's recommendation only came after Kyes had already turned down the position. But his worry about achieving a proper fit—namely, between the personality of whoever would chair the PAC and the decidedly political function that individual would have to play in building a robust coalition of bureaucrats and members of Congress—was spot on. As we saw in chapter 3, Clay in his capacity as chair of the PAC was an effective decision-maker who produced a highway plan well within the time frame that had been allotted to him by the president. At the same time, Clay exhibited all of the problems that Willis had anticipated Kyes would bring with him, and then some.

As a matter of legislative strategy, Eisenhower's perplexing decision to charge the preeminently nonpolitical Clay with the emphatically political task of persuading Congress to adopt a controversial highway bill is related to his previous (and equally perplexing) decision to pursue an aggressively executive-led highway bill in the months before a midterm election, the outcome of which was far from predetermined. Indeed, both decisions reflect thought patterns that seem to be emblematic of Eisenhower's leadership style in general. During the first two years of his first term, Eisenhower vacillated between using highway expansion as a means to secure and enlarge his present majorities in Congress, on the one hand, and relying on those same majorities to approve a highway bill that he would not otherwise be able to pass, on the other. By the time he settled on the latter alternative, he was heading into an uncertain midterm election, and there was simply no way he would be able to pass a Republican highway bill before the end of the 1954 session. Relatedly, Eisenhower had embraced Adams's plan to use an advisory committee of business leaders drawn from the private sector to break through the bureaucratic gridlock that had impeded meaningful progress on highway reform during the first two years of his presidency. Kyes and Clay—both men reputed for their uncompromising approaches to business, politics, and life in general—were clearly the battering rams by which Eisenhower and Adams anticipated being able to break through the hitherto stymied legislative process. Yet as personalities, both were ill-suited to the delicate work that would be needed to assemble congressional majorities in favor of highway expansion—even in a Congress with Republican majorities, where Eisenhower had consistently struggled to maintain a productive relationship with the GOP's conservative caucus.

"Budgetary Legerdemain"

When the Democrats won the House and Senate on November 2, 1954—roughly two months into Clay's tenure as chair of the PAC—it should have dawned on Eisenhower, the PAC, and everyone in his administration that their plan to pass a highway bill was in jeopardy. The most obvious new challenge would be securing passage of the administration's bill in all of the relevant congressional committees, which would now be controlled by Democrats come January 1955. By putting the process of designing highway legislation in the charge of four Republican businessmen, Eisenhower had not exactly ensured his administration's highway bill against criticism, or outright rejection, in the case of a Democratic victory in the 1954 midterms.

Yet the problems facing Eisenhower's highway bill ran deeper than the logistical question of which party controlled relevant congressional committees. During 1953–1954, Eisenhower's relationship with his own party in Congress had been tenuous, at best. Eisenhower observed early in his presidency that congressional Republicans, having spent the last twenty years in the political wilderness, were clearly accustomed to functioning as a minority and that they lacked the organizational capacity to act as an effective, forward-thinking majority.[3] Eisenhower's personal standing with the public gave him support that members of his party in Congress lacked, and Eisenhower's position as a political novice prevented him from either accessing or developing a robust political network in Congress, where many of his fellow partisans refused to support important pieces of his legislative agenda.

Structurally, things got even worse for Ike when the Democrats recaptured Congress. Unlike the GOP, whose internal chaos sometimes allowed Eisenhower to assemble bipartisan majorities of "Eisenhower Republicans" and internationally minded Democrats to support the administration's foreign policy, the Democrats possessed a strong, experienced, and nimble political network within Congress. Simply put, the Democrats had had the last two decades of New Deal hegemony to learn how to wield their majorities effectively, and as a political outsider, Eisenhower had no access to that network whatsoever. Further, his sporadic alliances with the Democrats on issues of foreign policy had likely accrued him a modicum of political goodwill, but Eisenhower had frequently clashed with congressional Democrats on matters of domestic policy. How his highway bill would be received by the new Congress was therefore far from certain.

Eisenhower caught a glimpse of things to come before the Eighty-Fourth Congress had even assembled. During December 1954, Clay had presented the outlines of the PAC's bill (hereafter, "the Clay bill") at several private-sector venues, including the American Municipal Association (AMA). These presentations were designed to generate interest in and support for the bill before Eisenhower formally asked the Congress to consider it. Accordingly, Clay's presentations were public, and although the precise details of his plan were not released until Eisenhower formally submitted it to the Congress on February 22, 1955, by January its basic features were becoming well known to everyone who cared about federal highways.

One of the most established figures in this area of policymaking was Senator Harry Flood Byrd Sr. (D-Va.), a staunch segregationist whose main legislative priorities besides maintaining white supremacy included roadbuilding and the federal budget. On January 18, 1955, twelve days after President Eisenhower announced in his Annual Message to Congress that he would be submitting a highway bill to Congress later that month,[4] Senator Byrd had a scathing critique of the Clay plan entered into the Senate Journal.[5] Byrd focused his attention primarily on the plan's financing mechanism, which Clay himself had admitted to be unusual, perhaps entirely unprecedented. As Byrd notes, the federal corporation that the Clay plan would create would have a contract with the Treasury Department according to which the latter "would guarantee the corporation's bonds." However, "the debt would not be included in the record of obligations guaranteed by the United States." Byrd then proceeds to spell out the absurdity of this proposal at length. According to the plan, Congress would be obligated to appropriate funds for repayment of interest and principal for the next thirty years. The Clay Committee claims that the bonds would not count as a debt against the Treasury, but what would happen if Congress decided to refuse to appropriate funds for repayment of the debt? Byrd observes, "The request could not be refused or reduced by subsequent Congresses, for thirty years, if the faith and credit of the Government are to be honored." In other words, a future Congress could well refuse to appropriate funds for repayment. Yet in practice their refusal would amount to a default: the federal government would be unable to repay a loan it had legally promised to repay. Byrd concludes his remarks on the Government Corporation with an overall indictment of the Clay Committee: "When the Government contracts a bona fide debt, but arbitrarily removes it from classification as public indebtedness, it creates fiscal confusion and disorder, and destroys confidence in Government credit. You cannot avoid financial responsibility by legerdemain, and you cannot evade debt by definition. The financial obligations of the Federal Government and all its citizens will remain." Biographer Ronald Heinemann contends that Senator Byrd was reputed to have an almost pathological—that is, irrational—aversion to debt, an aversion that is supposedly traceable to his experiences as a child in an excessively indebted family.[6] Regardless of whatever merit this characterization might have, Byrd saw to the very core of the Clay plan, and did the Congress and the general public a genuine service by clarifying just how illogical, not to say deceptive, its funding proposal was. What is more, Byrd's interest in the aspect of the plan that concerned funding was not merely a consequence of his general interest in fiscal policy; for the Eighty-Fourth Congress, he had been appointed chair of the Senate Finance Committee. Byrd knew that any proposal for funding highway expansion would need to pass his committee, and was therefore signaling his disapproval to the Eisenhower administration and to members of Congress who might be inclined to support highway reform. To that end, on February 17, 1955, Byrd wrote to the Comptroller General's Office asking about the nature and legality of the Clay plan's funding plan. In response, he received the following letter:

> Dear Senator Byrd: You inquired as to whether or not the Government has ever used a financing arrangement such as is proposed by the president's Advisory Committee on a National Highway Program in its report of January. That proposal called for the creation of a new Government corporation to be known as the Federal Highway Corporation and an authorization for it to issue bonds in an amount sufficient to cover the Federal share of the cost of constructing the proposed Interstate System of roads over a construction period of 10 years. While the terms and conditions of the Corporation's bonds would be approved by the Secretary of the Treasury and the plan calls for their repayment from funds provided by the Treasury as authorized by the Congress annually (presumably by appropriation action), the plan does not specifically provide that such bonds be guaranteed by the Secretary of the Treasury. However, all related factors plus the fact that they are to be issued by a Federal corporation would have the same effect. The total amount of such borrowing from the public would amount to $25 billion. The Corporation's activities would not be self-liquidating, it would have no important revenues, and funds for paying off the bonds would have to come from the general funds of the Treasury.[7]

Irrespective of his personal motivations for trying to torpedo the Clay plan's funding mechanism, Byrd's budgetary vigilance showed the Congress and the broader political system to be functioning in a healthy way.

Byrd's tactics also proved publicly effective: "Editorial writers across the nation echoed Byrd." Indeed, "to the *Nashville Tennessean* Clay's plan was a 'sham.' The Columbus, Ohio, *Citizen* termed it 'a gold brick scheme . . . which would hike the debt without acknowledging it.' The *Cleveland Plain Dealer* worried whether 'one session of Congress would obligate succeeding sessions to continue any appropriation.' The administration's bill never got beyond the Senate Public Works Committee. By the end of February it was dead."[8] Along these lines, on January 24, 1955, the *New York Times* ran an article discussing Eisenhower's highway plan. The article alleged that messages about highways and health care, which Eisenhower was anticipated to be sending to Congress in the next few weeks, were "expected to touch off major political controversies over the bills to put them into effect."[9] The article then cites Byrd's remarks in the Senate to substantiate this prediction: "The [highway] plan has already come under fire from Senator Harry F. Byrd, [who] said last week that the program would 'violate financing principles, defy budgetary control and evade Federal debt law.'" The *Times* takes care to point out that the highway plan in question was the work of Clay, a business elite: "The President's highway program is based on recommendations of a special study committee, headed by General Lucius D. Clay, retired, chairman of the board of the Continental Can Company." Despite overwhelming public support for highway expansion, Byrd's objections to the Clay plan's financing mechanism had already provided national newspapers with sufficient evidence that the administration's bill was likely to encounter significant resistance in the new Congress.

Revenge of the Nerds

At the same time that the Eisenhower administration was beginning to take flak from Byrd and others concerned about the Clay plan's problematic funding mechanism, the Inter-Agency Committee (IAC) and other members of the federal bureaucracy who had been sidelined during the process of legislative development in the fall of 1954 saw an opportunity to make hay with the PAC's proposal. Over the course of one month, from January 20 to February 17, General Bragdon wrote eight different memos for Arthur Burns describing in detail the machinations and controversies going on behind the scenes once Clay distributed his committee's plan to the administration. Unsurprisingly, Bragdon himself was not a passive observer.

The overall mood that would dominate these meetings was established at the very beginning of the first, on January 20, 1955, in Commissioner Du Pont's office at the Bureau of Public Roads (BPR). The meeting was led by White House congressional liaison Jack Martin, and attended by various members of the IAC and the BPR. Almost immediately, Martin was "surprised" when Du Pont and other highway officials "brought out that the Inter-Agency Committee had not been kept informed nor given advice to the Clay Committee; and also that the Bureau of the Budget and the Treasury Department felt certain serious matters in the report should be cleared up."[10] Given that the IAC consisted of members of Eisenhower's cabinet, including Treasury Secretary Humphrey (whom Eisenhower was friends with),[11] it is difficult to fathom how Martin could have actually been surprised that Clay had boxed out the IAC and the rest of the administration while he and the PAC members wrote their highway plan. The IAC had made their frustrations with Clay well known, and at one point had even threatened to withhold their support for whatever program the PAC produced. If Martin (and by extension, the rest of the White House staff) were in fact blindsided by this development, it was likely a consequence both of Eisenhower's well-known close relationship with Clay—no one, not even Humphrey, wanted to complain about Clay to Eisenhower—and of Adams's presence as a gatekeeper in the White House.[12] For his part, Adams had a personal stake in the outcome of the highway reform process; recall that he had squared off against Burns and Bragdon during the first stage of highway study, with Bragdon relentlessly criticizing the highway plan that Adams, with the help of Moses and Tallamy, had proposed. Further, it was Adams who in July proposed creating a President's Advisory Committee that would effectively sideline members of the government who had been working on highway plans all along. The Clay Committee (PAC) was Adams's brainchild, and he probably wanted to insulate the president from any criticism directed toward it by members of the federal bureaucracy who felt marginalized by Adams's plan.

Regardless of whether Martin and the president himself had known the extent of the animosity that had developed between the two committees, that animosity now threatened to derail any kind of cooperative relationship between the PAC and the rest of the administration who had not played a role in devising the Clay program. Part of the problem was that in following Adams's July 22, 1954, plan, Eisenhower had not given precise instructions regarding how the various officials who had already been involved in highway reform were to interact with the PAC once it had produced its plan. Nor had he given clear instructions as to the form that the Clay plan should take. Were Clay and the PAC merely generating ideas for a highway plan that could be hashed out by the administration and then by Congress? Or were they supposed to write an actual bill that could be sent more or less directly to Congress and contemplated for adoption? Was the Clay plan to be the final word on the subject? Or was it going to be circulated to and debated by the rest of the federal bureaucracy—including the members of the IAC, who by early 1955 were sour and looking for a fight because of Clay's intractability?

Regardless of what Eisenhower himself might have preferred, the members of the IAC and other federal officials (including Bragdon) chose to interpret the Adams's July 22 plan in the latter fashion. At the January 20 meeting, Marion Folsom, then undersecretary of the treasury (and future secretary of health, education, and welfare), stated that "the president's message should be very general and that the Administration itself should not draw up a bill but let Congress do that."[13] Unsurprisingly, Martin countered that "the message should be rather specific," but he also acknowledged that because "there were important matters in the [Clay] Report being questioned," perhaps it was not yet time to draft a concrete bill.[14]

The most important of these matters appeared to be financing. According to Bragdon, "frequent mention was made of Senator Byrd's opposition and ideas." Indeed, Byrd's objections appear to have reached Eisenhower's own comptroller general, who, according to Pearson, "had displayed opposition to the formation of a new corporation because of certain legal reasons."[15] On the same score, Bragdon himself observed that "there is a law which specifically mentions that the obligations of all Federal Corporations must be considered within the debt limit."[16]

These obvious problems appear not to have troubled the administration, however. In response to repeated comments about objections from Byrd—objections that should have been heeded, given that Byrd's Senate Finance Committee would have to sign off on whatever bill the administration submitted to Congress—Du Pont observed that a Mr. Anderson (Bragdon queries here: "Road Commissioner in Virginia?") had "attended the meetings of the Clay Committee and had spoken in favor of its plan." Du Pont appears to have believed that this fact belied Byrd's frequent public criticisms of the Clay plan, as if Byrd was not earnestly opposed to the Clay plan's funding mechanism. If he did believe this, he was sorely mistaken. Byrd remained a stalwart opponent of the administration's bill and helped secure its defeat in the Senate on multiple occasions.

Bragdon met with administration officials regarding the highway plan again four days later, this time with a significantly larger group that included Secretaries Humphrey and Weeks, Budget Director Hughes, and PAC secretary Frank Turner.[17] The increased size of the meeting itself seems to reflect growing awareness within the administration that the Clay plan had by no means settled the debate over highway legislation, that details over the highway bill were still very much up for grabs, and that anyone personally interested in the outcome of the process should therefore attend.

Bragdon begins his memo by observing that "there was much discussion as to how to handle the Clay Report; whether it should be forwarded as representing the president's views; forwarded merely as informative; not forwarded at all, but a message written outlining major points which were thought acceptable, and various other alternatives."[18] That the administration was pervaded by this degree of confusion at such an advanced stage of legislative development was a perverse consequence of Eisenhower's very desire to break through the logjam of competing interests that had traditionally hindered federal highway expansion. By concentrating the process by which the highway plan was devised outside the normal channels of legislation—indeed, by sidelining Congress entirely—Eisenhower had simply delayed until the very last minute deciding how to persuade Congress to adopt his plan. Matters had only been further complicated by the results of the 1954 midterms. And it did not help things that, because the process had taken so long as a result of these unanticipated sources of confusion, the team was forced to delay sending the president's message to Congress, missing Eisenhower's deadline (which he had announced in his January 6, 1955, annual message) of January 27. In trying to act decisively, Eisenhower had inadvertently created an organizational mess that forced him to draw out his own legislative process and miss his own self-imposed deadline, all of which gave the strong impression of indecisiveness.

With these problems in view, Eisenhower's highway team—if such a chaotic and mutually antipathetic group can be appropriately called a "team"—was debating whether the best course of action was to suddenly involve Congress at this late stage, or to press on with the original strategy and, in effect, present Congress with a fait accompli. Soon it became apparent that neither alternative was particularly propitious. According to Bragdon, the group decided that "very probably Mr. Martin and Governor Adams should discuss the matter with congressional leaders that would handle it. He stated that the congressional forces generally expect a bill as a point of departure for them to work on."[19] This report is unsurprising; members of Congress generally do want to have significant input regarding any bill they agree to sponsor, after all. What is surprising is the idea that the president would present Congress with the Clay plan merely "as a point of departure for them to work on," when the basic rationale for creating the PAC to come up with a plan all along was to circumvent the thicket of congressional pressure points. What exactly had been the point of the PAC in the first place?

The team was unable to resolve this contradiction. After deciding that the president should propose his plan as a mere point of departure, they proceeded to agree that the plan should be fully drafted by Du Pont, then vetted by both the Treasury Department and the Budget Bureau, and, finally, examined at a "preliminary meeting in the White House" (presumably with the president), all before meeting with "the Congressmen of the Committee and Subcommittee who will handle the matter." Why would they spend this much time drafting and vetting the proposal if it was only going to be dissected and reconstructed in Congress, assuming the relevant Democratic-controlled committees decided to consider it at all? The answer would seem to be that, even if Congress was going to scrap the plan the president chose to submit, each part of the highway group—especially important entities such as Treasury, Commerce, and the Budget Bureau—still wanted to have their say over whatever plan he ended up settling on. Put negatively, no one wanted to fail to put their imprimatur on the president's proposal in the off chance that, retrospectively, they might have been able to influence the final product in a way that helped their department or personal interest at the expense of someone else's.

At a third meeting, on January 27, Bragdon expressed his frustration at Clay's unwillingness to consider alternative funding mechanisms. Specifically, Bragdon was unable to comprehend why Clay and the others were unwilling to consider his own preferred method of funding: toll roads. Fumed Bragdon, "I am exceedingly disturbed on this subject of toll roads. I do not believe American people should be saddled with a $31 billion debt, $11 ½ billion of which is interest, if the roads could be gotten for nothing."[20] Bragdon had consistently advocated for toll highways throughout his involvement in highway reform, only to be rejected on the grounds that dense population centers would be unduly burdened by toll costs and that imposing tolls on previously free highways would be unpopular with the public. Characteristically, Bragdon failed or refused to appreciate these objections and continued to press for tolls even after Clay submitted the PAC's plan to the administration. Bragdon "furiously sent memoranda to Clay urging adoption of his position for a limited toll road system," states Lewis. "But Clay had also heard from du Pont, [Frank] Turner, and the Bureau of Public Roads on the matter and would have nothing to do with it. 'Dear Stuart,' wrote Clay in November, misspelling General Bragdon's name, 'I am afraid that our Committee does not believe toll roads to be the answer, nor do we think a national network of toll roads to be desirable.' Rebuffed, Bragdon lapsed for a time into sullen silence."[21]

That silence had worn off by January, at which point it had become clear that Clay's funding proposal was by no means a settled issue. To his credit, by placing so much emphasis on toll roads, Bragdon was attempting to thread the needle Eisenhower had presented to his highway team when he had announced that his administration wanted to significantly expand highways without adding to the federal debt *and* without raising taxes. Toll roads would circumvent the need for borrowing, and they would also technically not be a tax, but they would require users to foot the bill for road construction. As the above quotation makes clear, Bragdon was particularly upset that the Clay plan would require taxpayers to spend a huge sum on interest on bonds; he does not appear particularly upset at the idea of creating a government corporation that would somehow issue bonds in the government's name without adding to the debt (but he did mention a federal law forbidding such practices at the January 20 meeting).[22] At the same time, it was not true for him to claim that highways could have been "gotten for nothing." Irrespective of the interest that borrowing would invariably incur, the *political* costs of imposing a toll highway system, in general, and tolls on densely populated urban centers that would bear the overwhelming burden of toll fees, in particular, would be immense.

Every alternative on the table during these last-minute discussions entailed significant upsides and downsides, yet it was a persistent feature of these discussions that each camp within the highway study group saw only the strengths of their own plan and only the weaknesses of the others. This outcome was to be expected within any political context, but it undermined Eisenhower's effort to circumvent the logrolling process that he was invariably going to encounter in Congress with a more decisive, streamlined process within his administration. Eisenhower attempted to circumvent Congress, but because he still wanted to incorporate aspects of the legislative process that Congress is better designed to handle—and better equipped to manage—than the presidency, he ended up importing what amounted to an inferior version of the legislative process into his own White House. The different and competing camps of his highway team—Bragdon, Clay and the PAC, the BPR, the Budget Bureau, and the IAC—produced exactly the kind of factionalized lawmaking environment that characterizes Congress, but without the procedures, norms, and institutional memory that makes Congress more effective at resolving factional conflict into a workable majority.

The highway team continued to struggle in the weeks after they missed Eisenhower's original deadline of January 17. Bragdon notes that when the group reconvened on February 1 in Adams's office—this time with Clay in attendance—the highway message distributed to them, which they were supposed to discuss, had been completely rewritten by Du Pont and the BPR: "Only one paragraph remained which went to the heart of the matter." Bragdon quotes the paragraph in question: "A sound Federal highway program can and should stand on its own feet with highway users providing the (total) dollars necessary for improvement in new construction. Underwriting of the (interstate) and Federal aid system should be based on the planned use of income from gas and diesel (oil) taxes, (augmented in certain instances by toll revenues)."[23] The wording of this statement suggests that revenue from gas and diesel taxes would be used to repay borrowed funds appropriated to begin building highways, and that funds would be borrowed based on the amount of tax revenue that the government anticipated it would be able to collect in the future. Yet the actual mechanism for borrowing and repaying funds—for example, a government corporation or simply borrowing against the US Treasury in the conventional manner—was unspecified. Immediately the group began discussing tactics for advancing the president's message, even before the message's content had actually been determined. Secretary Humphrey suggested that the administration should wait to draft a bill until after the president sent his message, presumably so that the bill might be tailored to fit public and elite reactions to the message.[24] Humphrey's approach would seem to require a vaguer, more general highway message, and need to invite more congressional participation in the actual drafting of the bill. This approach, though sensible for the reasons described above, was clearly a departure from the administration's general strategy so far, which had counseled creating the PAC as a means of breaking through congressional stalemate. The rest of the group sensed this departure and reacted accordingly: "[Humphrey's plan] was opposed on the ground that the administration should have a bill up promptly." Why had Clay and the members of the PAC spent months researching and drafting a specific highway plan if that plan was not going to provide the foundation for the administration's preferred bill? After all this, and to repeat, what had been the point of the PAC?

Clay himself echoed this concern when the subject of financing came up and toll roads were suggested. Likely piqued, Bragdon adds that "General Clay was very voluble in his opposition to tolls." Clay then proceeded to lay down the gauntlet: "If any other position was going to be taken in the legislation than [the PAC's] recommendation for financing with the gas and oil taxes, his report ought not to be sent forward." Adams, Bragdon's antagonist throughout the highway reform process, seemed "very favorable to all of Clay's remarks," and so "it was finally decided that in the administration's bill for legislation it be entirely as in the Clay report." In other words, Clay's proposal for a government corporation would be the funding mechanism on which the president's bill would be based. The meeting concluded after the group decided that Clay's temporary office in Washington, DC, would assist in drafting either the bill or the message or both—Bragdon's notes are unclear. Bragdon also notes that it was agreed that Clay would "assist in working with Congressmen in getting the bill through."

As of February 1, Clay had again taken charge of the highway reform effort, this time with the help of Adams, who had helped steer the Clay proposal through the rocky shoals of the IAC and the extended federal highway network. Clay's funding mechanism would remain the core both of the president's message and of the administration's bill, and Clay would play a crucial, if not authoritative, role in drafting the bill and negotiating with members of Congress. Why the highway group felt that assigning the politically inexperienced Clay, "the Great Un-Compromiser," the task of whipping votes in Congress made strategic sense is far from clear. For the time being, however, the administration had decided that it would double down on the Clay plan instead of inviting Congress to view the administration's bill as a mere jumping-off point.

Eisenhower was apprised of these developments after the February 1 meeting and, sometime between then and February 7, authorized a subcommittee of the PAC to handle public relations for the highway program. In so doing, Eisenhower was deepening his commitment to the general idea that, rather than involving congressional leadership in the actual process of developing a highway plan, pressure for his administration's concrete highway bill should be exerted on Congress by White House and private-sector officials. On February 7, Eisenhower phoned Clay to ask if the subcommittee had been set up, and Clay responded that it had, but he felt it best that the group not be assembled "unless there was some specific problem to take up."[25] Having just tousled with the IAC and the broader federal highway network at the February 1 meeting, Clay was clearly hesitant to convene any more committees unless there was a clear plan on the table; he did not want more open-ended debate over the plan that had already been deconstructed by the IAC. Eisenhower agreed, and went on to suggest that "there were a number of ways Senator Byrd's opposition to highway program could be countered—by steel companies, labor unions, cement companies, etc."

Eisenhower's response to the growing public threat from Byrd is striking. Instead of meeting and negotiating with Byrd directly, Eisenhower wanted to outflank the vocal deficit hawk by rallying the various industrial interest groups who would benefit from government contracts necessitated by a massive highway expansion program. Eisenhower appears to have believed that pressure from these groups on members of Congress would be weighty enough to overcome Byrd's influence on the Senate Finance Committee (which would invariably be involved in whatever funding mechanism was proposed). He also appears not to have been troubled by the prospect of resistance on the part of congressional Democrats who regarded $11.5 billion in bond interest as a boondoggle for Wall Street, who resented having been cut out of the legislative process entirely, or both.

In two meetings following Eisenhower's conversation with Clay, nearly a month after Eisenhower's original deadline of January 17 for sending a highway message to Congress, the president's highway group was still debating basic details about the administration's highway plan. After February 1, the group's focus turned from the funding mechanism to the organization of the highway authority that the proposal would create. Unsurprisingly, Bragdon favored a centralized, top-down model headed by a single director unencumbered by a committee, the BPR, or a dense bureaucracy and answerable directly to the secretary of commerce.[26] Also unsurprisingly, senior members of Eisenhower's cabinet objected to this model and argued for a structure that would be decidedly subordinate to one of the major administrative departments. Secretary Humphrey and members of Treasury lobbied for "a strong Commission which would be over the executive [of the highway authority]."[27] Bragdon thought "they were wrong in this point of organization," and at one point stated in his memorandum that "it looked almost as if we were right at the beginning as far as organization was concerned." He humbly adds that "it sustains the wisdom of my initial proposition that these major matters should be settled first before any attempt at details were gone into."[28] While self-congratulatory, Bragdon's observation is also on the mark. At the very least, the point of the PAC would seem to have been to settle on a general structure so that minor details might be hashed out later on between Clay and the president or in Congress. Eisenhower's felt need to involve senior administration officials who had been immersed in highway policy with the Clay plan at this point in the game was an attempt to both introduce deliberation into a process that might otherwise be excessively myopic and mollify the feelings and interests of members of his administration who had been sidelined from the process of actually drafting a highway plan. The result was protracted disagreement between these officials, each of whom wanted to reconstruct the bill in a way that accorded with their particular interests and goals.

The need to actually settle on a plan that could be sent to Congress—lest the already protracted internal debate over the administration's proposal drag on further and result in the same kind of stasis that had overwhelmed highway reform during the summer of 1954—appears to have been felt most acutely by Commerce Secretary Weeks, whose department would likely have had to supervise whatever highway authority the administration proposed creating. "Because of the confused state that [the highway proposal] was in," observes Bragdon in his February 10 memorandum, "Secretary Weeks called General Clay and General Clay discussed the matter with Governor Adams and also with Mr. du Pont and finally directed Mr. du Pont to write the draft up on [*sic*] accordance with the Clay Report." After nearly a month's worth of meetings and controversies, the president's highway group decided to simply send the Clay report, which had been finished since December.

The Gore Bill

On the morning of February 16, 1955, at his weekly legislative conference, Eisenhower took the first concrete step of his administration to involve Congress with his highway project. In a confidential memorandum to Budget Director Hughes summarizing the meeting, Staff Secretary Arthur Minnich states that "the President's Message to Congress on [the subject of highway legislation] will be preceded by appropriate coordination with the interested Committees on a bipartisan basis."[29] Each of the three senior Republican legislators present—Styles Bridges, chair of the Senate Republican Policy Committee; Charles Halleck, former House Majority Leader; and William Knowland, Senate Minority Leader—reacted favorably to General Clay's "brief presentation" of his plan. At the same time, each anticipated that the Congress would want to be involved in drafting and modifying specific components of the administration's bill, including "the Government's financial commitment," the tax burden carried by truckers, and how highway routes would be apportioned among the states.[30]

The most important point mentioned at this meeting, however, was that Eisenhower would be meeting with "interested Committees on a bipartisan basis." To repeat, it had been purposefully decided in the preceding days that the president would be sending the complete Clay plan to the Congress, as opposed to an outline of the administration's broader highway goals, which would have signaled an invitation for Congress to become involved in drafting its own bill. Because Eisenhower clearly was not trying to send this signal, and was instead trying to get Congress to adopt the concrete plan he was endorsing, it is therefore difficult to understand what Eisenhower and his senior officials believed they would accomplish in a bipartisan meeting held shortly before he sent his administration's bill to Congress. Perhaps the president genuinely believed that by inviting the Democratic leadership to the White House and thereby signaling his goodwill, he could convince them to adopt his administration's bill. But from a political standpoint, it seems naïve to believe that members of the opposing party—now in control of Congress and therefore in a position of relative strength—could be persuaded to open their minds to, let alone embrace, the opposition's bill in the course of a single afternoon, especially given that they had been completely marginalized from the process of developing that bill in the first place.

Nevertheless, on Monday, February 21, the day before the president forwarded the Clay plan to Congress, Eisenhower held an afternoon meeting in the White House Cabinet Room with the chairs and ranking members of the congressional Public Works Committees—Dennis Chavez (D) and Edward Martin (R) in the Senate, and Charles Buckley (D) and George Dondero (R) in the House—and with chairs and ranking members of the Subcommittees on Public Roads—Albert Gore Sr. (D) and Francis Case (R) in the Senate, and George Fallon (D) and Myron George (R) in the House.[31] Also in attendance were Clay and Adams. The meeting went exactly how Eisenhower should have anticipated. According to James Hagerty, who took notes, the president opened the meeting with some very general and uncontroversial remarks about the need for expanded federal highways on the basis of increased traffic, national defense, and economic development.[32] He then became more specific, asking the committee members to take seriously the plan Clay and his committee had created before having Clay give a brief presentation of his plan. Notwithstanding Senator Byrd's already familiar criticisms of the plan's funding mechanism, Eisenhower described the plan as a road program that "will not add to our national debt."[33] Characteristically, the president ended his remarks by asserting that "our approach should be above politics."

Senator Chavez opened for the Democrats by expressing his appreciation of Eisenhower's goodwill, and then stated his party's commitment to the general platform of highway expansion. But in the same sentence, Chavez hints at the problem that anyone familiar with the highway debate that was then unfolding should have been familiar with: funding. He states that although "we do not differ on the meed [sic]" for highway expansion, "we may differ about financing or other matters." After Clay outlined his plan, both Chavez and Gore asked why it was necessary to pay $11 billion in interest in order to raise funds. Gore stated that the money used for paying interest could instead be used to pay for roads. Once again, the issue of financing had hamstrung the broader enterprise of highway reform.

Two features of this meeting are significant for understanding and evaluating Eisenhower's decision-making process. The first is more straightforward, and is rooted in the incoherent logic of the strategy for highway expansion that he pursued throughout his first term.

Eisenhower began his remarks at the February 21 meeting as if he were speaking to members of Congress at the very outset of negotiations, establishing basic sources of common ground, professing a willingness to operate on a bipartisan basis, and indicating his openness to a variety of alternative policy proposals. The problem with his message was that it was deeply misleading. Ike was in fact coming to these members at the very *end* of negotiations; he and his administration had spent the better half of his first term in office negotiating among themselves about a concrete highway proposal. As a result, the Democratic committee chairs saw the meeting and the Clay plan for precisely what they were: not an open-ended invitation to argue and negotiate about a highway bill, but rather an already complete highway plan that was the product of a quasi-legislative process from which they had been entirely excluded. Rhetorically, matters were only made worse when Eisenhower stated at the end of his introductory remarks that he was going to send his message to Congress "tomorrow." If everything else said before had not already established the fact, this statement confirmed Eisenhower's motivations. There was no way for the Democrats to change the bill in a meaningful way with less than one day to spare. And even if there were, Eisenhower had made it clear that he was not inviting them to alter the Clay plan: "I would be the last to say there are no errors or mistakes in the plan but I will say that we must push ahead on it."[34] The president was not seeking the Democrats' input; he was presenting them with a finished plan that he evidently expected them to endorse.

Once it become clear that the Democrats were less than enthusiastic about the Clay plan and the overall status of highway reform, a shift in the general mood of the room can be gleaned from Haggerty's editorial in his notes: "About the only good that came out of the meeting that I saw was that the president was on public record of asking for bi-partisan consultation on the program. The only good was this doodle which the president did while the meeting was going on."[35]

It is unclear whether Eisenhower decided to host congressional Democrats merely to give the misleading impression of bipartisanship to the public, or if this remark was merely Haggerty's attempt at salvaging some value from an otherwise pointless meeting. If it was indeed the former, the calculation was strange because it was widely known, thanks to Senator Byrd's frequent public criticisms, that the PAC had finished its work more than two months ago. What is more, Eisenhower himself had announced in early January that he was planning to send a message to Congress later that month. Clearly he had missed his own deadline, and a zero-hour meeting with congressional Democrats presumably would not have persuaded anyone that the process had been bipartisan. What we can say with some certainty is that once it became clear that the Democrats were unwilling to accept the Clay plan as it stood, Eisenhower basically lost interest in the discussion. Haggerty gives no indication that Eisenhower said anything else before abruptly leaving the meeting after about an hour of conversation.[36]

Eisenhower's February 21 meeting was bizarre on a deeper level. During an exchange between Clay and Senator Chavez, Senator Gore had taken issue with the Clay bill's funding mechanism, which would have required paying $11 billion in interest. According to Haggerty's notes, Clay responded that his plan "was the best program that he could figure out and that as far as he was concerned, Senator Gore's plan would not work for the simple reason that (1) the Governors were against it and (2) that the states did not have monies available to match the $1.6 billion which Gore was proposing."[37] Haggerty notes that the meeting ended with Gore and Chavez saying they "were going to press for their own program."[38]

If it comes as a surprise that Gore and Senate Democrats had been working on their own highway bill all this time, it should. Albert Gore Sr. of Tennessee had served in the US House of Representatives for fourteen years before successfully running for Senate in 1952. Gore wrote to Senate minority leader Lyndon Johnson in early 1953 stating his preferences for the Appropriations, Agriculture, and Foreign Relations Committees.[39] Instead, Johnson put him on Public Works, where Gore immersed himself in important infrastructure concerns, such as the Tennessee Valley Authority and the Atomic Energy Commission.[40] He also involved himself in highway policy. On February 11, 1955, while Clay, the IAC, and the broader federal highway network were still haggling over the president's message to Congress, Senator Gore introduced Senate Bill 1048. Indeed, "even before Eisenhower had submitted the Clay recommendations to Congress [on February 22, 1955], Gore had announced hearings on his own highway bill."[41] Gore's plan differed from Clay's in that it proposed spending a smaller amount of money—

$10 billion—in a shorter period of time: through fiscal year 1961. In addition, the Gore plan would have had the states match 25 percent of federal funds instead of the Clay plan's 10 percent—hence, Clay's assertion that the state governors would oppose his plan and that the states would not have enough money anyway. Gore's plan did not include a funding mechanism, because all spending bills must originate in the House.

It is unsurprising that Gore's bill differed from Clay's. After all, in the course of two years the Eisenhower administration had produced numerous competing plans that differed from one another in significant details. What *is* surprising is that, in the wake of the 1954 midterms, neither Eisenhower himself nor anyone in his administration appears to have made any effort to establish contact with members of the House and Senate Subcommittees on Public Roads to inquire if there was already a highway program in the works. Further, even once it became clear that Gore had beaten the administration to the punch with the submission of SB1048 on February 11, Eisenhower's highway team continued to debate the Clay plan as if nothing had changed. Clay's remarks at the February 21 meeting indicate that he was certainly aware of the Gore bill—indeed, that he had read it with enough care to understand how it differed from his own. Presumably, the others who attended that meeting had done so too. Yet Haggerty's notes suggest that the president simply spoke to Gore and the other Democrats as if the latter did not have a highway bill of their own.

Consistent with his decision-making thus far, Eisenhower appears to have believed that it made more sense to simply press forward with his administration's bill than to attempt to reconcile the Clay plan with Gore's. Yet as a matter of broad strategy, this decision is hard to rationalize because the two plans had much more in common than we might have expected. Both dramatically increased federal highway spending; the only major differences were matters of degree and not kind, for example, should states match 10 percent or 25 percent. Moreover, the Gore bill did not even specify a funding mechanism, which meant that there was even more room for the administration and congressional leaders to negotiate. Presumably there was a solid basis of agreement on which Eisenhower could have hashed out smaller differences with congressional Democrats and Republicans.

Yet as before, here too Eisenhower had boxed himself in as a consequence of previous tactical decisions. Instead of consulting with congressional Democrats after the November elections in order to gauge interest in highway reform, the president simply doubled down on the Clay plan and committed himself to sending his administration's proposal to Congress by January 27 in his 1955 Annual Message. Thus, when news of the Gore plan reached him in early February, it was too late to substantively change course. He was already weeks late sending his administration's bill to Congress, and suddenly involving Congress at this advanced stage in the process would give the impression of indecisiveness, even chaos. His choices were, therefore, to abandon the commitment he had made in his Annual Message and suddenly involve Congress—thereby undoing roughly seven months of preparations and negotiations—or to honor his own commitment and move forward with his own bill as if the Senate had not already begun contemplating a bill of its own. He chose the latter.

On February 22, the president submitted his administration's highway message to Congress. The message contained three elements: the Clay plan, a BRP study made by the Eighty-Third Congress, and Eisenhower's brief of the Clay plan and the general principles of his highway vision. Eisenhower's brief and the Clay plan existed in considerable tension with each other. As he had been doing since his late-1952 Hearst announcement in *Road Builders' News*, Eisenhower here describes the need for highway expansion in general and noncontroversial terms, emphasizing current traffic conditions, the deleterious state of present roads, national security, and the interconnectedness of roads and the national economy.[42] Relatedly—and unsurprisingly—he points out that the current arrangement and trajectory of roadbuilding under the Federal-Aid system was inadequate to present and future needs—"At the current rate of development the interstate network would not reach even a reasonable level of extent and efficiency in half a century"—before summarizing the BPR's estimate of how much money would need to be spent within a given extent of time in order to remedy the problem.[43]

So far, none of what Eisenhower was saying would have raised many red flags in Congress. He was describing the nation's roadways in an uncontroversial manner, and making the case that roads were a national problem because national as opposed to purely local concerns—highway fatalities, national security, and the economy—depended on the nation's roads. Accordingly, when he came to the part of highway reform that had proven most controversial—funding—he was tentative. As before, he began by stating that the highway program should "stand on its own feet"—that is, that it should be funded by revenues from the highway system itself and not by general tax revenues. This proposition alone is unproblematic, but it raises the question of how funds will be increased in order to meet rapidly growing highway needs. After all, the main defect of the current arrangement (the Federal-Aid Act of 1954) is not simply that it raises insufficient revenue, but that it raises revenue too slowly to meet present and future needs. The problem is how to raise an enormous amount of funding, enough to execute a massive expansion of highways, in a relatively short period of time. Accomplishing this end required choosing between two—and only two—alternatives: either preserve the current arrangement and simply raise user taxes in order to fund more building projects, or borrow the funds in order to launch the project and pay back the bonds through future user revenue, which would increase significantly as more drivers are able to use the new roads.

Following the Clay plan, Eisenhower proposes the latter, but in so doing he both hesitates and obfuscates: "I am inclined to the view that it is sounder to finance this program by special bond issues, to be paid off by the above mentioned revenues which will be collected during the useful life of the roads and pledged to this purpose, rather than by an increase in general revenue obligations."[44] This statement makes it sound as if Eisenhower is simply proposing to issue bonds that will count against the national debt. Of course, anyone familiar with the Eisenhower administration's fiscal policy would have known full well that, even compared to raising taxes, further debt spending was anathema to the president's convictions. Clearly the president was not proposing to simply raise the federal debt in order to pursue highway expansion.

And in fact he was not, as Senator Byrd had made abundantly clear on his public criticisms of the Clay plan's idiosyncratic funding proposal. For his part, Eisenhower ends his message by acknowledging the complexity of the funding problem and only half-heartedly endorsing the Clay plan: "Inescapably, the vastness of the highway enterprise fosters varieties of proposals which must be resolved into a national highway pattern . . . [the Clay plan and the BPR study] provide a solid foundation for a solid program."[45]

There are two basic problems with this otherwise statesmanlike message. The first concerns Eisenhower's less than forthright endorsement of the Clay plan's funding plan. There was a clear tradeoff that had to be faced between increasing user taxes or borrowing. And in order to be addressed credibly, the tradeoff had to be presented to the Congress and the public in a principled and honest way. If Eisenhower wanted to borrow, he needed to explain why building new roads in a short period of time was worth forcing the general public to pay billions of dollars in interest to those who purchased highway bonds, instead of paying for the roads themselves and nothing extra by means of tax increases. This position is neither prima facie right nor prima facie wrong; rather, it needs to be justified on the basis of a reasoned explanation of the relative importance of economic equity and the nation's transportation needs. It also requires explaining why highways are important enough to require adding to the nation's debt and thereby violating Eisenhower's commitment to a balanced budget. Likewise, if the president believed that raising user taxes was a less desirable alternative to borrowing, he needed to explain why forcing the public to pay interest on bonds in the long term was better for the country than forcing the public to pay more in taxes in the short term, without having to pay any interest whatsoever. Was Eisenhower genuinely convinced of the soundness of his funding proposal, or did he see it as a kind of magic trick that would allow him to simultaneously expand highways and claim his administration had not added to the debt? Gore hinted at the latter in an interview with *Transport Topics* following his February 21 meeting with the president: "Sen. Gore, one of the conferees, reported after the White House discussion that he had questioned the president closely on how the Administration could spend the money as proposed and maintain that it would not increase the national debt. He said that Mr. Eisenhower smilingly agreed it would be a debt, but it would not [be] part of the national debt."[46] Was Eisenhower's smiling response to such a serious question the equivalent of a wink, intended to establish an unspoken understanding, or rather an unintended nervous response to Gore's forceful line of questioning?[47]

88   CHAPTER FOUR

The second problem, a tactical one, was a consequence of Eisenhower's overall flawed legislative strategy. Eisenhower described the Clay plan as a "foundation" for a highway program. In fact, as the flurry of contentious meetings during January and February confirm, Clay's proposal was a fully finished product—not just a foundation, but a fully constructed building, complete with walls, roof, and interior. The message was all the more obtuse because Congress knew full well that Senator Gore had been working on his own highway bill at least since February 11, when Gore formally submitted SB1048 to the Senate. Why would Eisenhower speak as though he was open to a range of alternative highway plans, and not acknowledge that Congress was already at work on their own?

Despite its conciliatory and open-minded surface, Eisenhower's highway message wreaked of disingenuousness. By presenting Congress with the Clay plan, Eisenhower was clearly not inviting the legislators to build on an admittedly incomplete structure, but instead presenting them with the finished product and asking them to vote up or down on it. Further, in speaking as though he were inviting Congress to build their own highway bill on the broad foundation of his message, Eisenhower was running up against the same problem he had encountered in meeting with congressional Democrats the previous day. There was a patina of deliberativeness and bipartisanship to the ordeal, but the plain facts signaled that, far from soliciting their input, Eisenhower wanted Chavez and Gore to give the Clay plan a rubber stamp. When they refused, he had no other choice but to press forward with his plan, even though it was clear he was going to fail.

And fail he did. In the weeks following his message, Eisenhower's highway plan met with a barrage of criticism, the most devastating of which came from within his own administration. On March 18, Senator Byrd appeared before Senate Subcommittee on Public Roads, chaired by Senator Gore. The committee held its first meeting on February 21—the day before Eisenhower's highway message—and continued to meet until mid-April. In general, the committee did a remarkable job of clarifying the nature of the Eisenhower plan and, in particular, exposing the contradictions that had been built into it as a consequence of its tortuous path through the executive branch. During his March 18 testimony,

Byrd recapitulated his criticisms of the Clay plan's finance mechanism, calling it "legerdemain" and delivering what the *New York Times* called "a jolting blow to the Eisenhower Administration's highway-building plan."[48] Specifically, Byrd contended that "the interest charges would be much too heavy" and "that the proposal was 'incapable of honest Federal bookkeeping and accounting.'"[49] The *Times* article notes the strange fact that although Byrd was "frequently an Administration ally in money matters," nevertheless he was appearing before the committee "to attack the [administration's] highway plan." Byrd's objection of course was that the Clay plan *would* add to the debt, and that Eisenhower was failing or refusing to make the hard decision he needed to make: borrow funds or raise taxes.

Things kept getting worse for the administration in the days that followed Byrd's testimony. Five days later, on March 23, the *Times* ran an article, "Humphrey Offers Rise in 'Gas' Tax: Informs Senators He Would Accept Increase to Help Pay for Highways."[50] This article was an embarrassment for the administration, which had gone on record being against tax increases. Secretary Humphrey made these remarks during testimony before Gore's committee the day previous, on March 22. According to the *Times* article, "the Secretary appeared in support of the Eisenhower program . . . and ran into a barrage of questions that indicated the Administration proposal was in serious trouble." When pressed about the Clay plan, Humphrey seemed to contradict Byrd's allegations and "denied that the bond plan was 'a trick to avoid the debt limit.'" Yet shortly thereafter, he stated that "he would not object . . . if the Congress sees fit to increase the Federal gasoline tax in order to finance this program." Then, in an even more dramatic reversal, Humphrey announced that "he would not be opposed to revising the public debt statement . . . to include the proposed highway bonds." The *Times* then quotes Humphrey directly: "I'm in favor of having the debt statement revised to show everything we owe, if it were possible to do so . . . because I think it's good for people to know just what they do owe."

These admissions amounted to an implicit reversal in the administration's policy and directly undercut the president's plan, which was an effort to avoid raising taxes and above all an attempt to avoid adding to the debt. In his official capacity, Humphrey had expressed his openness to both of these. In effect, then, Humphrey had mimed a defense of the Clay plan while signaling his support for a completely different alternative, one the president had rejected. Why might he have done this? It seems possible that as head of the agency that would have to oversee the Clay plan's proposed government corporation, Humphrey actually shared Byrd's concerns about the feasibility and legality of issuing bonds that would not count against the federal debt. Indeed, weeks later in April, Humphrey would appeal privately to Byrd in an attempt to convince him to support a toll road alternative to Clay's beleaguered plan.[51] Humphrey had also been part of the IAC, which had been marginalized from the initial drafting process of the Clay plan; doubtless he, like Bragdon, was still upset from his rough treatment by Clay. At the very least, we can say that by expressing his support for a mode of financing explicitly discouraged by Clay and the president himself, Humphrey made a point of not giving the Clay plan his unwavering support. This development might have made sense had Eisenhower actually invited Congress to explore a range of possible highway plans—it would have signaled Treasury's openness to considering alternatives, too—but it seemed strange for one of the president's cabinet officials to not fully support the concrete plan that the president himself had made a point of insisting on.

As least as far as his own administration was concerned, the nail in the coffin of Eisenhower's highway bill came on March 28, when the US comptroller general testified before Gore's committee. As head of the Government Accountability Office, established by the Budget and Accounting Act of 1921, the comptroller general functions as the federal government's highest accountant, monitoring government income and expenditures. One of the comptroller's chief responsibilities is to verify the legitimacy and legality of government borrowing. Eisenhower's comptroller was therefore one of the most qualified government officials to testify before Gore's committee about the Clay plan's funding mechanism. The comptroller general has a term of fifteen years, and is nominated by the president. Accordingly, on December 14, 1954, Eisenhower replaced Lindsay Carter Warren with Joseph Campbell as comptroller general; previously, Campbell had served as Columbia University's treasurer, where he and Eisenhower had become acquainted.

Whatever sense of loyalty Campbell might have felt toward Eisenhower from their Columbia days did not extent to his understanding of the Clay bill's proposed government corporation. At the March 28 hearing, Senator Stuart Symington—filling in for Senator Gore, who was absent—asked Campbell to give the General Accounting Office's opinion of SB1160, the Eisenhower administration's highway plan.[52] It is worth quoting the relevant passages of Campbell's testimony in full:

> [The Eisenhower bill] would create a new Government corporation to be known as the Federal Highway Corporation. The Corporation would be authorized to issue obligations not to exceed $21 billion. . . . We feel that the proposed method of financing is objectionable because the result would be that the borrowing would not be included in the public debt obligations of the United States. While the issuance of the Corporation's bonds would be with the approval of the Secretary of the Treasury and the obligations would be repaid from the permanent appropriation . . . the obligations would specifically state that they are not obligations of, or guaranteed by, the United States. . . . Both of these provisions coupled with the permanent appropriation would apparently be to assure the investors of ability to meet obligations, and tend to have the effect of a Government guaranty of the highway obligations, at least in the mind of the investing public. As a practical matter, the obligations would be moral and equitable obligations of the United States, since they would be issued by a Corporation entirely owned by the Government.[53]

In language that borrows almost directly from Senator Byrd's critique, Campbell states that "the Government should not enter into financial arrangements which might have the effect of obscuring the financial facts of the Government's debt position." Then, echoing Secretary Humphrey's testimony from March 22, Campbell states plainly that "the highway program—since it, in reality, is nonrevenue producing—should be financed by appropriations made by the Congress."[54] In the course of the question period that followed Campbell's presentation, the comptroller evinced additional reasons to reject the Clay plan's proposed corporation. In response to Republican senator Edward Martin's request for further information about the "limitations" of the proposed corporation, Campbell asked Robert Long, director of the General Accounting Office's Audit Division, to elaborate on the point. Long states that "wherever possible, in the establishment of any corporation, the Congress should spell out as distinctly as possible the powers or the duties which the corporation is to perform. As the chairman will recall, there have been a number of corporations that have been formed to perform specific functions and as the years went by, they become engaged in many programs that were not intended or desired by the Congress."[55] Not only would the corporation obscure the extent of the federal government's debt obligations, which was undesirable enough. Because the bill committed Congress to permanent appropriations of the company without giving Congress explicit means to enforce the corporation's compliance with the highway law's mission, the Clay bill effectively created an autonomous government agency with the authority to raise money in its own name. As both Senator Martin and Assistant Comptroller Long were making clear, the potential for corruption, fraud, and mission to creep in the proposed company was boundless.

The slow churn of Gore's committee had unearthed before the Senate and the broader public serious problems built into the Eisenhower administration's poorly constructed plan. It exposed contradictions, especially concerning the financing mechanism, that were rooted in the PAC's tensions and conflicts with the IAC and the administration's broader highway network. Through testimony from Eisenhower's treasury secretary and comptroller general, it unearthed sources of skepticism and doubt within the administration itself—the very officials who would be responsible for administering and overseeing the implementation of the Clay bill were it turned into law. Perhaps most impressively, it channeled the individual ambitions of the key players involved, including Byrd and especially Gore, in a publicly desirable direction. No doubt motivated by his legislative goals as a partisan of SB1048—his own highway bill—Gore created the conditions for a sustained, and ultimately devastating, public analysis of the Clay plan's proposed funding mechanism.

In turn, testimony before Gore's committee helped clarify and bring to public attention what the Clay plan's government corporation truly was: not a borrowing plan that would somehow still honor Eisenhower's professed commitment to fiscal responsibility, but a government boondoggle for investors who stood to make more than $11 billion in interest and that concealed a massive government loan behind dishonest rhetoric. Indeed, the overlapping concerns between Senator Byrd and Comptroller Campbell attracted the attention of the Democratic National Committee, which in April circulated a fact sheet detailing problems with the Clay plan and suggesting the superiority of Gore's alternative. One of the fact sheet's principal takeaways was that "financing the highway program outside of the debt ceiling [had been] criticized by Sen. Byrd and Ike's Comptroller General as 'obscuring financing facts' and 'creating fiscal confusion and disorder.'"[56]

Perhaps the clearest indication of the plan's dishonest nature was Eisenhower's own March 30, 1955, press conference. Merriam Smith of the United Press asked the president: "What do you think of the position taken by the man you nominated as Comptroller General in opposition to your highway program? He has told the Congress that he thinks the financing system is unsound and, possibly, illegal."[57] Eisenhower's response revealed more through what it did not say than through what it said explicitly:

> Well, Mr. Smith, I nominated to the position of Comptroller General the man I thought was best qualified in the United States. Mr. Campbell was my associate and assistant when I was at Columbia University. He was the treasurer of a very large organization. He is a splendid accountant, and he is certainly an honest gentleman. Now, the last thing I would ever ask any man that I appoint to high office is what are going to be his decisions in specific cases. If any man would pledge to me that he was going to make a certain decision because I asked him, he would never be appointed. So have to concede to him his right to follow his own judgement and convictions. But I do tell you this, I think he is wrong. [Laughter][58]

Why was he wrong? On the basis of what understanding of budgetary law and government accountability was Campbell mistaken about the Clay plan's government corporation? Here we glimpse in bold relief

Eisenhower's ability to use his authority and amiable disposition to evade a relevant question about the basic nature of one of his favored policies. Given his mum response to Mr. Smith, the paucity of any developed justification for the government corporation in his highway message to Congress, and the absence of any sustained discussion of the matter in his journal, correspondence, or White House records from this time, it is not unreasonable to wonder if Eisenhower had given any thought to the feasibility or legitimacy of the government corporation whatsoever.

A letter from Eisenhower to Paul Helms dated April 30, 1955, suggests as much.[59] The front page of the April 30, 1955, *New York Times* reported: "Senate Unit Votes 5-year Road Plan; Bars a Bond Issue. Ignores President's Request on Financing—Asks Cent Rise in Gasoline Tax."[60] The subcommittee had voted in a bipartisan majority of 6-3 to send the Gore bill (SB1048) to the Committee on Public Works for a full vote. According to the *Times*, "Mr. Gore predicted that the Public Works Committee would report it next Thursday [May 5] and the Senate would pass it the following week." Likely having read the *Times* article that morning, Eisenhower angrily penned to Helms that "measures, obviously designed for the welfare and advancement of the whole country, [had been] blocked by partisanship and selfish personal reasons." The president appears completely oblivious of all the reasons why the Clay bill might strike some—including members of his own administration—as falling somewhat short of "obviously designed for the welfare and advancement of the whole country." Indeed, likely because they too had been completely excluded from the bill's drafting process, even the congressional Republicans who "introduced the [Clay] bill as a courtesy to the president" nevertheless "gave it only token support."[61] The responsibility of advocating the bill on the Senate floor was taken up by Republican senator Prescott Bush (R-Conn.)—father of George H. W. Bush and grandfather of George W. Bush—who was then in his second year of office, having won a special election in 1953. Bush, who "had earned a fortune working for the investment banking house of Brown Brothers, Harriman, and Company," likely comprehended how much money there was to be made on interest payments from bonds issued by the Eisenhower bill's proposed corporation.[62] Unfortunately, Prescott Bush was less lucky than his grandson would be forty-five years later. This round of Bush versus Gore went to the senator from Tennessee.

When the Senate took up the Gore plan later in May, Senator Martin, ranking member of the Public Works Committee and a member of the Subcommittee on Public Roads, proposed on May 25 to substitute the Eisenhower bill for the Gore bill on the grounds that the highway building plan proposed by the latter would take too long to complete.[63] The previous day, Martin had met with Eisenhower, the congressional GOP leadership, and other senior administration officials to discuss how to counter the Gore bill,[64] which the Senate had begun considering in the preceding four days, on May 20. A May 24 confidential memorandum from Staff Secretary Minnich to Budget Director Hughes states that "it was agreed that every effort should be made in the Senate to substitute the Martin bill [i.e., the Clay plan] for the Gore bill. If that should fail, efforts should be concentrated on returning the Gore bill to Committee or finally disapproving it in order that the path may be cleared for Senate consideration of the Administration proposal following House action on it."[65] As Mark Rose observes, the Eisenhower administration was confident that notwithstanding Senate resistance to the Clay plan, the House would be more open to it—ranking House Public Works Committee member George Dondero "believed that the Administration bill would be reported without difficulty in the next week or ten days by the [Committee on Public Works]"[66]—and that the administration would therefore be able to leverage a successful House floor vote to put additional pressure on the Senate.[67] At this point, Eisenhower's strategy was less about passing the Martin bill—though he clearly wanted that attempted—and more about simply stalling the Gore bill.

The bearish remarks by GOP congressmen present at the May 24 legislative conference should have been a clear indication of the small likelihood the administration's strategy would succeed. Senator Martin notes "recent suggestions in the Senate" that, among other things, "a different method of financing than was recommended by the Administration" should be considered. Senate minority leader Knowland too reported concerns about the Clay plan. Neither of the Senate's two senior advocates of the administration plan seemed particularly confident about their chamber's receptiveness to that plan. And by airing the grievances of other senators, they were likely trying to insulate themselves from criticism once the administration invariably failed. Yet Eisenhower was undaunted. In response to Knowland, who like his Senate colleagues Byrd and Gore "was concerned with the possibility of saving interest charges by avoiding the issuance of corporate bonds," Eisenhower, Hughes, and Humphrey "stressed the desirability of avoiding any addition to the national debt in connection with the highway program."[68] Notwithstanding the remarks of his own comptroller general, Eisenhower appears to have still believed that the government corporation's bonds would somehow not count against the national debt. And given Knowland's commitments as a conservative Republican, the only alternative left on the table—raising taxes—was out of the question. Speaking as a former governor who appeared to be unaware that passing the highway plan at this point required convincing Congress, and not the state governors, Adams ended discussion of the highway bill by "emphasiz[ing] the necessity of keeping faith with the Governors and hence for avoiding any suggestion of an Administration willingness to compromise on important aspects of the program."[69] It was therefore decided that, notwithstanding their minority in the Senate, and lukewarm support from congressional Republicans, Martin and Knowland would press ahead with the Clay plan.

The next day, May 25, Martin moved to substitute Eisenhower's bill for Gore's. In response to the motion, Senator Chavez pressed home the point that by this time had gained significant public and elite traction, as reflected in Senator Knowland's remarks in the previous day's legislative conference:

> I know the provisions of the administration bill contain much gain for those in the road construction industry . . . [and] there is plenty of gain in the proposed administration bill for those who would invest in the program as it is outlined in that bill, to such an extent that the investors would make $11 billion out of a $21 billion investment. . . . A profit of $11 billion on a $21 billion investment certainly is not in keeping with the conscience of the American people. Deep in my heart I feel that way because I have seen state-

ments published in investment journals to the effect that the so-called administration bill would be good for the investors.

In response, Martin pressed Chavez on how the Gore bill would finance highway expansion. Chavez deferred to Gore, who responded that his bill did not provide a source of revenue and that if it were to borrow the funds, it would borrow less than the administration bill would.[70]

After a full day of debate, the Senate voted on the Martin amendment to substitute the Eisenhower bill for the Gore bill. The amendment failed 31–60, with five members not present or abstaining.[71] Of the thirty-one senators who voted for the Eisenhower bill, thirty were Republicans. All forty-seven Democrats voted against the amendment, as did thirteen Republicans, who defected from Eisenhower. Of those thirteen, eight were from states where both senators voted against the administration bill: Nebraska, Idaho, North Dakota, and South Dakota. These rural states likely would have benefited more from Gore's bill, which apportioned more highway mileage to rural states than did the Eisenhower bill. Of the five remaining GOP senators, John Butler of Maryland and William Jenner were anti-Eisenhower Republicans who had supported McCarthyism.[72] Similarly, Andrew Schoeppel of Kansas had supported Robert Taft instead of Eisenhower at the 1952 Republican Convention.[73] Frederick Payne was a Republican in liberal Maine who would lose handily to Democrat Ed Muskie in 1958. And John Williams of Delaware was a well-known deficit hawk,[74] who likely opposed the Eisenhower bill because of its finance mechanism. After rejecting the Eisenhower bill, the Senate approved the Gore bill in a voice vote, signaling its overwhelming popularity.[75]

Crash and Burn

The April 30 *Times* article and the May 25 Senate votes were not unalloyed good news for Gore and his highway allies, however. The April 30 article concludes with a section titled "House Approval Doubted," and states that "there were no assurances that the House Ways and Means Committee, which had original jurisdiction, would approve the gasoline tax increase recommended by the Senate subcommittee. Prospects for favorable action, in fact, appeared slim." Per Article I, Section 7, Clause 1 of the US Constitution, all revenue bills must originate in the House of Representatives. Gore had succeeded in writing a bill that would allocate funding, but he needed the House to decide how that funding would actually be raised. This fact was relevant to Congress's highway program because, unlike the Senate, the House has to confront the issue of appropriations in addition to actually drafting and marking up legislation in committee. The House Ways and Means committee normally has the responsibility of addressing financing concerns, while other relevant committees consider the substantive content of the bill in question.

In the case of any highway project, the obvious choice for moving a bill through the House was Democratic Public Works Committee chairman George Fallon, a "known quantity" in Congress and highway circles who was "a longtime supporter of public road initiatives" and who had "always worked in a bipartisan fashion on the issue."[76] Fallon held hearings on a House highway plan from April 18 until June 1, shortly after the Senate vote. Before the Senate approved the Gore bill, all accounts "suggest that Fallon's subcommittee was seriously considering the Clay Committee's plan." During the May 24 legislative conference, Representative Dondero had anticipated that the House Public Works Committee would report out the Eisenhower bill: "However, when the Senate soundly rejected [the administration's plan], Fallon began looking for an alternative."[77]

Unsurprisingly, given his connections to the broader federal highway and roadbuilding network, Fallon turned to Frank Turner, assistant to the public roads commissioner, for help in drafting a new highway bill, one that actually stood a chance of passing the Senate. Turner, another "known quantity" in the roadbuilding field, was a highway expert with decades of experience in government service.[78] What is somewhat surprising about the Fallon–Turner connection is that Turner had been appointed by Eisenhower as executive secretary of the PAC, where he appears to have had minimal influence over the committee's report.[79] With the PAC effectively dissolved as of May 1955—Clay was not present at the May 24 legislative conference, for example—Turner appears to have been free to lend his expertise to Fallon and House Democrats, who were looking for an alternative to the now dead-in-the-water Clay bill.

The process by which the Fallon bill came to a vote in the full House during the spring and summer of 1955 was idiosyncratic in several respects, but from the standpoint of Eisenhower's decision-making process, one consideration in particular warrants scrutinizing: time. As of early 1954, Clay and others in the administration were confident that the Eisenhower bill would have the support of the House, and that the administration could in turn leverage that support to apply pressure to the Senate, which was known to have serious reservations about the administration's plan. Evidently, the administration did not anticipate that the Senate would act so quickly in rejecting the Clay plan and substituting the Gore bill in its place. On the eve of the vote for the Gore bill, Eisenhower appeared genuinely confident that his bill would receive the support of the Senate, or at the very least that it would not be voted down. House highway officials appear to have shared the president's confidence, with Dondero anticipating successful passage in the House and Fallon holding hearings on the administration plan during the preceding months. As a consequence of the Senate vote, forward legislative momentum suddenly swung toward the Gore plan, thereby creating the pressure for the House to propose a plan that at once satisfied the Senate and that would not be vetoed by the president.

What this meant for Fallon and the House leadership was as follows. If a highway bill was going to pass the House and the Senate before the end of the Eighty-Fourth Congress's first session on August 2, the House had to draft, hold hearings on, and pass a bill satisfactory for the Senate and the president in under two months. For all of the coalitional and partisan reasons we have been describing so far, this was no easy task. Had the House leadership choreographed more carefully with Gore, Chavez, and Majority Leader Johnson during the spring of 1955, the House would likely have been in a position to pass a bill acceptable to the Senate soon after the May 25 Senate vote, with both chambers negotiating their differences in conference committee and presenting the president with a finished bill well before the summer recess. For his part, Eisenhower would have been institutionally well positioned to help coordinate this kind of effort. Sensing the Democrats' skepticism of his administration's bill during the early weeks of 1955, he might have used his February 21 meeting with congressional Democrats to ensure cooperation between the two chambers over a mutually agreeable highway package. Instead, he squandered the opportunity by using that meeting to obtusely insist the Democrats endorse a highway bill they, along with members of his own administration, had been vocally criticizing in the preceding weeks and months.

Despite the unfavorable timing, Fallon was still committed to passing highway legislation and began working on a new bill once it became clear the Senate would not pass the administration's plan. Yet the constrained time frame forced Fallon to make two decisions that hamstrung his efforts. First, he reached an agreement with Speaker Sam Rayburn that allowed his subcommittee to write significant tax changes into the bill.[80] Setting tax policy is normally the responsibility of the powerful House Ways and Means Committee, which like all congressional committees jealously guards its authority against outside encroachment. Why Rayburn and Fallon felt this decision made strategic sense is unclear, but they likely feared that involving Ways and Means would unnecessarily protract the process and prevent the bill from being passed before August. Allowing Public Works to write the tax provisions instead would streamline matters without producing a substantively different bill. Second, the constrained time frame limited the number and length of committee hearings, which created an impression of hastiness and prevented interested members from hearing relevant testimony for and against the bill.

These two decisions antagonized the constituencies whose support the bill needed in order to stand a decent chance of passing. After Fallon reported out his bill to the full Public Works Committee on July 28, the bill's proposed tax increases immediately touched off a controversy among highway users, especially truckers and automobile organizations, who were going to bear the lion's share of the bill's new tax burden. In turn, the vocal negative reactions of these groups convinced Public Works "to assign a new subcommittee under Fallon to formulate a new plan."[81] According to Rose, the new committee "produced only a scaled-down version of Fallon's original proposal." Fallon's subcommittee recommended increases in "the Federal gasoline tax to 3 cents a gallon, instead of 2 cents; diesel fuel to 6 cents from 2 cents; heavy truck tires, 15 cents a pound instead of 5 cents; and heavy truck tubes, 15 cents instead of 9 cents. A new tax of 7 ½ cents a pound on retreaded large tires was recommended, along with a proposal to increase the excise tax on trucks to 10 percent from 8 percent."[82] Once it went back to Public Works for consideration, the already weakened revised Fallon bill was then kneecapped by the Ways and Means Committee, whose members were indignant for having been excluded from writing the bill's tax components. Sidelining the Ways and Means Committee was a risky decision on Rayburn's part; at this time, the Ways and Means Committee also served as the Committee on Committees, which gave it full authority over committee assignments of all House members.[83] By alienating Ways and Means, members risked losing the committee assignments they most desired and receiving ones that would be useless to them.

When he gave Fallon's subcommittee the authority to write the funding components, Rayburn therefore allowed Ways and Means to send some of its members to sit in on hearings,[84] which began on July 11. And although those members could question witnesses and participate in debate, according to Representative Hale Boggs, a Ways and Means member, they were not authorized to actually vote on the final bill, Rayburn likely fearing that these resentful members would use their votes to prevent the bill from being reported out. Rayburn's instincts were sound. For example, Republican committee member Richard M. Simpson used this modification of House custom to vocally protest the bill: "We sit here unhappily without a right to vote on the matter of who is to pay for the tax."[85] Indeed, rather than placate Ways and Means, Rayburn's concession appears to have only further antagonized them: "That this agreement might not be satisfactory to the Ways and Means Committee was reflected in seemingly petty disputes over which door its members would use to enter the hearing chamber and where they would sit during the hearing."[86]

Fallon's bill also failed to garner the support of the president, who on June 29, the day after Fallon introduced his bill, commented on the development during his news conference. Asked about the Democrats' "plan to finance long-range highway building by drastic increases in taxes on tired and also gasoline," Eisenhower responded that there were three alternatives: (1) "very greatly increased taxes," (2) a bond issue that would add to the national debt, or (3) a bond issue "under a special organization in which liquidation is provided for, and which will get this whole sum of debt off our books as rapidly as possible."[87] Having expressed his continued support for the Clay plan's discredited funding plan, Eisenhower then argues against raising taxes on the grounds that doing so would deprive the states of their revenue sources. He concludes his response without clearly indicating his disposition toward the Fallon bill, simply reiterating his support for the administration bill.

Mixed messages also came from Treasury Secretary Humphrey,[88] who testified before the Public Works/Ways and Means hybrid committee on July 12. In a seeming course correction from his position during testimony before the Senate committee in March, Humphrey endorsed the Clay plan while also expressing his own openness to "any equally effective program which the Congress sees fit to adopt for the construction of highways with sufficient additional tax levied to pay as we go."[89] Like Eisenhower, Humphrey appears to have been muting his approval of the Fallon bill in the hopes that the moribund Clay plan might be resuscitated. Rather than endorse a highway bill that, although differing in significant respects from the Clay plan, nevertheless greatly expanded federal highways without violating the president's principle of not increasing the debt, Eisenhower and Humphrey withheld their support so as not to undermine the administration plan, which stood no chance of passing the Senate whatsoever.

Like the Ways and Means Committee, highway user organizations (especially trucking and automobile associations) likely felt that House leadership was trying to sneak the Fallon bill and its significant tax increases by them without their input or consent. As a consequence, "petroleum, tire, trucking, utility, and labor interests were among those who testified and lobbied the Members [of the hybrid committee] behind the scene."[90] These interest groups also protested publicly, with members of the American Transportation Association parking a semitrailer covered in dollar bills in front of the Capitol. In addition, members of Congress reportedly received around 100,000 telegrams during this time.[91]

Despite the consternation of these groups, Speaker Rayburn evidently still felt confident about the bill's prospects. On July 19, the Public Works Committee approved a slightly modified version of the Fallon bill, which was then scheduled for a floor vote to be taken on July 27. Rayburn stated publicly that he was "violently opposed" to the Eisenhower bill, which Republicans were still trying to substitute for the Fallon bill, and that he believed the Fallon bill "should pass the House all right."[92] Senate leadership appeared confident also; in that chamber, there were "plans to speed the bill through the Finance and Public Works Committees."[93] Yet the Fallon bill still had to be passed by the House Rules Committee, which had authority to decide how bills would be debated on the floor and, specifically, whether bills would be subject to floor amendments. Here again, the unconventional process of the Fallon bill, made necessary by its urgency, was felt by everyone who had a stake in its outcome. "Normally, the Rules Committee would forward a revenue package from the House Ways and Means Committee to the House under a 'closed' rule," forbidding amendments on the floor.[94] But because the entire Fallon bill, including the revenue component, had been written by Public Works, Ways and Means wanted to amend the revenue portions on the floor so as to include their input, which had been left out during the bill's original drafting by Public Works. For his part, Fallon obviously wanted the revenue portions sent to the floor under a closed rule to prevent Ways and Means members and other interested parties from altering the portion of his bill that he and Rayburn had worked so hard to preserve. After negotiations, the Rules Committee sent the bill to the floor under a "modified open rule" that allowed floor amendments to every part of the bill except for the revenue portion, to which only members of Public Works would be permitted to propose amendments.[95]

On July 26, the House voted 274–129 to consider the Fallon bill the next day, July 27, under the modified open rule allowing three hours of debate time. When the House began debating, Republican members, following George Dondero, moved to substitute the administration's bill for the Fallon bill. Democratic representative Patman took the lead in recapitulating his party's objections to the Clay plan, stating that "the Clay committee was weighted down with investment bankers, commercial bankers, brokers of Government bonds." More pointedly, he asserts: "It seems as though every proposal that is offered for schools or roads, they [the administration] begin first by finding out how many bonds are to be issued, for what period of years, and what the interest rate will be. It seems that the first consideration is the bankers and what they get out of it and not the roads, not the schools."⁹⁶ Given that Eisenhower's first concrete step toward supporting highway expansion back in December 1952 had been to ask investment banker Walker Buckner for a bond proposal, Representative Patman was more correct in his accusation than he likely realized.

The House rejected the motion to substitute the Clay bill by a vote of 221–193, largely on party lines. Every indication was that the Fallon bill, which was to be voted on next, would pass by a similar margin, if not greater. But as the roll call was taken, it became clear the bill was in serious trouble, and even an eleventh-hour endorsement by Adams sent to a Republican member of Congress was unable to push it over the edge.⁹⁷ "When they started calling the roll alphabetically," Turner said in a 1988 interview, "out of about the first 50 names there was one vote in favor of the bill. All the rest of them where against the bill."⁹⁸ The Fallon bill died by a vote of 292–123, and with it, any hope of highway expansion in 1955.

CHAPTER 5

The Final Push and Congressional Victory

> *The politics of American highways has always been dominated by one overwhelming truth: everyone loves roads, but no one wants to pay for them.*
> —Theodore H. White

It would be both uncharitable and inaccurate to blame President Eisenhower and his administration for the House's failure to pass a highway bill in July 1955. Decisions made by George Fallon, Sam Rayburn, and other individuals within House leadership and committees were hardly within the president's control. Moreover, the Senate had added another hurdle to the process by resoundingly defeating Ike's plan on May 25, which action had the effect of dramatically constraining the range of potential legislative outcomes. And yet, key decisions by Eisenhower starting at the very beginning of his presidency and up until the July 27 House vote made passing a highway bill before the 1955 summer recess significantly more difficult than it might have otherwise been. Before examining the process by which a highway bill was finally passed in 1956, it is worth reflecting briefly on how the most important decisions Eisenhower made regarding highway legislation during 1952–1955 might have affected the fate of the Fallon bill.

Squandered Opportunities

Beginning with his decision to seek extensive input from investment banker Walker Buckner before his term of office even began, Eisenhower consistently sidelined the Congress as a whole and even members of his own party within Congress, preferring instead to concentrate efforts on designing a highway bill within his White House and administration. These efforts were stymied from the outset for want of clear directions and in-fighting between members of Eisenhower's staff. Irrespective of the content of the various competing programs that emerged as a consequence of this not infrequently contentious process, Eisenhower himself was unable to settle on a coherent legislative strategy for pushing ahead with highway expansion. Would federal roadbuilding projects serve as a means to increase Republican majorities in Congress in the 1954 midterms, so that a more ambitious highway program might be passed subsequently? Or, would the president use the congressional majorities he already had before the 1954 midterms to pass a highway bill, a bill that might fail were the Democrats to recapture either houses of Congress in 1954? By the time Eisenhower decided to push for legislation in a more aggressive way—organizing the business-oriented Clay-led PAC in later summer 1954—the midterms were already looming, and it was unclear whether the GOP would retain its majorities in either chamber. And when the Democrats did, in fact, recapture both chambers in November, it should have been clear that whatever plan the PAC proposed was unlikely to receive a warm welcome by any of the relevant committees (a proposition that was validated almost immediately when, shortly after the November elections, Senator Harry Byrd, the soon-to-be Finance Committee chairman, publicly excoriated the Clay plan).

Starting in January 1955, then, Ike was at a crossroads. Facing Democratic majorities in Congress, he could have invited the input of Gore, Fallon, and other members of Congress who were concerned with roadbuilding, either in the hopes of pursuing a truly bipartisan highway plan or, more pragmatically, as a way to make passage of a highway bill more likely in Congress. Alternatively, he could press forward with the Clay plan in hopes that the Democrats would receive it favorably, or, at least, that the Republicans might be able to peel off enough Democrats in both houses to assemble a modestly bipartisan coalition. He chose the latter.

In February and March 1955 it became clearer that the Clay plan would face considerable opposition in both the House and Senate. Senator Gore submitted his own highway bill early in February, and a perfunctory meeting with congressional leadership in late February made it clear that the Democrats had no interest in the administration's plan. In April and May, as the summer recess grew nearer, it was evident that the White House and Congress were working at cross purposes, and that it was going to be difficult to reach an agreement satisfactory to all parties involved at all, let alone within two or three months. Thus, when the Senate overwhelmingly (and unsurprisingly) voted down the Eisenhower plan at the end of May, Eisenhower and congressional Democrats had a little more than two months to reach an agreement about a legislative problem that had stymied presidents and Congresses for decades before. But instead of taking necessary precautions, such as soliciting the input of congressional Democrats, Eisenhower continued to press for his own plan and refused to even signal his openness to an alternative presented by Congress.

This was the situation the House and its relevant committees had found themselves in as of early June 1955. George Fallon, the House's leading highway legislator, had less than two months to design a bill that would satisfy Eisenhower and the Senate. To do that, the bill could neither borrow funds and increase the national debt, nor, per the Clay proposal, issue bonds using a government corporation. The latter would be rejected by the Senate, whereas the former would be vetoed by the president. Additionally, whatever bill the House settled on would have to appropriate enough funding to expand highways far beyond current capacities—an enterprise that would require tens of billions in taxpayer dollars.

Given these constraints, the only logical choice was to raise taxes. Yet even within the House itself, there were real impediments to passing a new funding mechanism within a shortened time frame. The powerful Ways and Means Committee would normally have drafted the revenue package, but because those hearings would have dragged out the process, Fallon wanted Public Works to have sole control. Drafting a highway bill by August also required dramatically expediting hearings from powerful user organizations, who, as a consequence, felt they were being rushed and that their concerns about the increased taxes were being shunted aside. Eisenhower only endorsed the Fallon bill on the day of its scheduled vote moments before the roll call began, which left the House leadership no time to build a stronger coalition.

By attempting to derail the Democratic plan, and withholding his support of that plan until the very last minute, Eisenhower effectively forced the House to expedite a process that would normally have taken many months of preparation. Indeed, on the same day as the July 27 vote on the Fallon bill, allies of the administration were still vainly trying to replace the latter with the Clay bill. Not only were Fallon and his allies expending capital trying to assuage the concerns of highway users and the Ways and Means Committee, they were also wasting time and energy trying to beat back the Eisenhower administration's allies in Congress. That Eisenhower decided to endorse the Fallon bill when it was too late is therefore intensely ironic. Had Ike expressed openness to a Democratic alternative in the House back in May, when the Senate made it clear it would never accept the Clay plan, he would have at least opened up more room for the House to consider the Fallon plan on a relatively normal timeframe, without having to rush through the important process of writing a tax program and thereby alienating its most important constituencies. Better yet, the president might have expressed greater openness to the Gore bill in February, thereby creating the pressure for House and Senate leadership to collaborate on a bill with plenty of time for both chambers and their relevant committees to hold hearings and mollify their constituents.

"No Chance—None Whatsoever"

On July 27, after the Fallon bill was defeated, Speaker Rayburn told a *New York Times* reporter that "the people who were going to have to pay for these roads put on a propaganda campaign that killed the bill." Rayburn was seconded by Republican leader Joseph Martin, who had "a sneaky idea that the truckers of the country played an important part in" defeating the legislation. What is more, "legislators said privately that they had been subjected to unusually heavy pressure by truckers and others fighting the tax increases."[1] By withholding support from the Fallon bill, Eisenhower had done nothing to insulate the House from these pressure groups. Indeed, in the days preceding the July 27 vote, a member of the PAC, Dave Beck of the Teamsters Union, instructed his truckers to discourage their members of Congress from voting for the Fallon bill because of the user tax increases.[2] Regardless of whether Beck was operating on his own or at the behest of Clay, whose highway committee he had previously participated in, it demonstrates a remarkable lack of coordination on Eisenhower's part that a member of his own highway committee would try to sink a highway bill that actually stood a chance of passing Congress, all while his own bill was dead on arrival.

On July 28, the president urged the House to reconvene and try again to pass a highway bill, but he was sternly rebuffed by Speaker Rayburn, who sensed correctly that there was no appetite in Congress for reconsidering any of the bills that had failed to pass in the preceding days: "President Eisenhower," wrote John D. Morris of the *Times*, "voiced hope today that Congress would revive a road-building program before adjournment. 'No chance—none whatsoever,' was the response of Speaker Sam Rayburn."[3] Astutely, Rayburn recognized that relitigating the highway debate again during the few days that remained before the summer recess would not solve anything, for the essential problem that had killed the Fallon bill was not its content, but the manner in which that content had been presented to the House and the broader public. In attempting to rush through Congress the largest public works project in the country's history, House leaders had failed to secure the consent of that project's most interested parties. What was needed if the bill was to succeed was not another attempted sprint to the finish line, but a full and transparent review of the bill's financing proposal by everyone concerned, precisely the kind of activity the Congress—and the House in particular, in which all revenue bills must originate—is designed to conduct.

For his part, even in his public statement urging Congress to reconsider highway legislation, Eisenhower failed to support the Fallon plan, merely stating that he had submitted a plan he felt to be "sound," and conceding that "others have proposed other methods." Given that Rayburn, a Democrat, had supported the Fallon bill, and, further, that the Fallon bill had garnered significantly more support than had the administration bill, there would appear to have been no good reason for Eisenhower to believe that Rayburn would have been inclined to take up the matter again unless, at the very least, he had been assured of Eisenhower's support. Once again, Eisenhower appears to have believed that simply chastising the Congress—"I am deeply disappointed by the rejection by the House of Representatives of legislation to authorize a nation-wide system of highways"—was enough for him to fulfill his presidential duties.[4]

In the weeks that followed, and notwithstanding Minority Leader Martin's public statement that the president would be on "solid ground" to convene a special session of Congress for purpose of pursuing highway expansion, Eisenhower came to the conclusion that successful legislation would be highly unlikely until at least the next session of Congress.[5] During his press conference on August 4, Eisenhower was twice asked if he was considering convening a special session to consider highways, and twice he replied that he had made no decision at that time.[6] David Sentner of the Hearst Newspapers followed up by asking if, in the case the president did call a special session, he would be proposing a new highway plan, that is, one that differed from the Clay plan. Eisenhower began by acknowledging that "I did say in my original recommendations that I recognized there could be more than one method of financing, but at a time when we wanted definitely to allocate certain user type of money to the paying of those roads, we needed the roads now, and when Congress very definitely and I think maybe a lot more people do not want to raise the public debt, there remained one method: the corporation or the authority method. And that is the one I proposed."[7] This statement is misleading in an obvious way. Eliminating a proposal to use deficit financing did not leave only one financing method on the table, for the Fallon bill would have funded highways by raising taxes instead of adding to the existing debt. Eisenhower is speaking as if the Fallon alternative simply did not exist—indeed, as if raising taxes was not even a conceptual possibility, let alone the alternative that had garnered more support in Congress than his own financing method had. The president concludes his response: "I might accept some modification, of course I would. But what I want first of all is roads, and then a way to pay for it that will be acceptable and fair to the taxpayers." This seemingly open-minded profession is belied by Eisenhower's consistent refusal to support to Fallon bill and to acknowledge the challenge posed to the Clay bill by the Senate. Notwithstanding his attempts to reassure his audience of his nonpartisan position—"What I want first of all is roads, and then a way to pay for it"—Eisenhower's seemingly dogged commitment to the Clay plan's bogus financing proposal, which had been rejected by members of his own administration and laughed out of the Senate, signals that he was more concerned with the way of paying for roads than with the roads themselves.

Perhaps unsurprisingly given his previous prevarications regarding the Clay plan's government corporation, Treasury Secretary George Humphrey appears to have been one of the first members of the administration to recommend abandoning the government corporation altogether. He also urged a better legislative strategy. In a memorandum dated August 16 from Humphrey to Sherman Adams (one of the Clay plan's chief partisans), Humphrey recommends getting to work immediately on a new highway proposal to be ready by October 1955.[8] He states plainly that he is "convinced that there is no chance to finance a program as was previously proposed [in the Clay plan]." He urges the administration to ready a new proposal as soon as possible because he anticipates "an enormous amount of spade work will have to be done... with responsible members of Congress" in order to prepare the ground for a second consideration of highway legislation. Finally, Humphrey states that there is no "chance in the world for success with a complete package proposal handed to Congress after it convenes on a take-it-or-leave-it basis."

Humphrey's memorandum is a wholesale repudiation of every aspect of Eisenhower's strategy for highway expansion so far. Unlike Ike, he recommends jettisoning the discredited government corporation and simply borrowing or raising taxes to pay for new roads. Unlike Ike, he suggests reaching out directly to the members of Congress who will be directly involved with the bill, in order to maximize the likelihood of a smooth legislative process. To that end, he proposes having a proposal ready to go early on so that plenty of time remains in late 1955 and early 1956 to meet with congressional leadership. Finally, unlike Ike, he notes that whatever plan is presented to Congress cannot be a finished product but rather must be only a basic structure, open-ended enough for the House and Senate to build out according to their preferences.

Eisenhower's Heart Attack and the Weeks Committee

On September 24, 1955, Eisenhower suffered a heart attack while vacationing in Colorado. Though there were no pressing national emergencies at the time, Eisenhower's cabinet decided that it would be advisable for them to hold regular meetings to ensure continuity of government while the president recovered.[9] On September 26, Secretary to the Cabinet Maxwell Rabb sent Adams a memorandum advising that the cabinet meet regularly during the president's convalescence "to emphasize to the whole country that we have a team here in smooth continuous operation."[10] Per Rabb's suggestion, an agenda for a September 30 cabinet meeting was distributed on September 29; item 3 on the agenda was the interstate highway program.[11] According to the same agenda, an announcement was to be made "of a new Presidential Advisory Committee to be composed of Secretary Weeks [of Commerce], as Chairman; Secretary Humphrey; Secretary Wilson [of Defense]; Secretary Benson [of Agriculture]; and Governor Adams, with [White House Congressional Liaison] Jack Martin as Secretary." The agenda adds that the president has approved of the formation of the new committee, which will "look over past history, will work at a later stage with General Clay's committee and with Governor Kohler's committee, and will then determine what the administration's highway program should now be."

The next day, during the September 30 cabinet meeting, Adams proposed forming a new highway "administrative group, particularly since Gen. Clay's illness prevented him from resuming work."[12] The new committee would "report to the Cabinet" and would "decide what, if any, changes [to the administration's highway program] should be recommended this year." Adams also observes that the state governors had appointed a new highway committee that would be meeting on November 3.

These developments signal the intervention of Secretary Humphrey in the highway program, an intervention made possible especially by Clay's absence from the scene. Humphrey's August 16 memorandum to Adams had argued that, given recent developments in Congress, the Clay proposal needed to be overhauled if not abandoned entirely if the administration's highway plans stood a chance of succeeding. Accordingly, the new committee reflected Humphrey's vision, and his own institutional goals, in three important respects. Whereas the original committee structure had put Clay in the driver's seat, with the Inter-Agency Committee (IAC) (of which Humphrey and Weeks had been members) in a subordinate role, the new arrangement reversed the order in which a new highway plan would be considered; this time, the Weeks Committee would be in charge of formulating the plan, with the PAC in a secondary (and merely advisory) capacity. This organizational change is underscored by an October 6 memorandum from Max Rabb to President Eisenhower that specifies that "a *New* Presidential Advisory Committee [had been] set up."[13] This phrasing indicates that the Weeks Committee was not merely an additional study group meant to supplement Clay's efforts; it had in fact replaced the PAC as the new advisory committee.

Second, the members of the leading committee would be members of the administration, not officials from the private sector. The leading committee would therefore reflect the priorities of the agencies that would be in charge of administering whatever plan was finally authorized by Congress.

Finally, the Weeks Committee would report directly to the cabinet. As noted previously, General Clay was especially close with Eisenhower, and he seems to have had outsized influence over the White House legislative process at the expense of other interested officials, including Weeks, Bragdon, and especially Humphrey (who, as we have seen, was only a reluctant advocate of Clay's bond financing proposal). Having the Weeks Committee report directly to the cabinet allowed it to circumvent the president's intimate relationship with Clay. We might go so far as to conclude that the illnesses of Eisenhower and Clay nevertheless opened up space within the administration for hitherto marginalized officials, such as Humphrey, to bring a new perspective to the problem of highway legislation.

The new committee got to work immediately, with an October 1 White House "Record of Action" stating that the Weeks Committee would review both the Clay proposal and "Congressional action taken on it."[14] This statement suggests that, unlike previous attempts at highway legislation by the administration, the Weeks Committee would attend to the concerns of Congress and particular congressional committees, where highway legislation would need support in order to pass. On this score, Humphrey's August 16 memorandum to Adams emphasized the change that was most needed: scrapping the Clay plan's government corporation, which had been received with hostility by both houses of Congress. The October 1 record also specifies that the Weeks Committee would report its findings to the cabinet "prior to November 3," the day the new governors' committee was supposed to convene. This stipulation suggests that the committee wanted to preempt whatever highway proposal the governors' committee settled on, given that it was the Congress and not the state governors who would actually be voting on the final highway package.

The Weeks Committee worked through October, meeting with trucking companies to negotiate a tax deal that would persuade the latter not to pressure Congress the way they had in July.[15] In essence, the truckers did not oppose tax increases as such, only what they had perceived as inequities in the Fallon bill that had put an undue tax burden on truckers relative to automobile drivers. The truckers were fine with a 2 percent increase on truck excises "provided proceeds went straight to highway construction."[16] Having completed these meetings, the Weeks Committee met its self-imposed deadline of November and reported a general structure for a highway plan at the October 28 cabinet meeting.

Secretary Weeks led off discussion of the highway program, noting first that "the [Clay plan's] bond proposal had now been eliminated as a possibility."[17] Further, "the Committee recommended new or increased taxes so as to finance a $26 billion program . . . over a 15-year period." In accordance with their mission to review congressional action previously taken on highway legislation, the taxes proposed by the Weeks Committee were similar to those proposed by the Fallon bill while also reflecting input from truckers: "a 2¢ increase on gasoline, an increase on tires, a tax on camel back, and an increase of 2% on the excise tax on trucks and buses, bringing it up equal to the automobile excise." Humphrey concludes his remarks by emphasizing the need to preempt the governors' committee: "He wished to present this proposal to the Governors [sic] highway Committee on November 3rd and invite their concurrence or submission of an alternative proposal which would not depend on deficit financing." Past conflicts between the states and the federal government had frequently concerned the states' desire to retain revenue from gasoline taxes. The governors had supported the Clay plan because its proposed bond financing scheme would have left state gasoline taxes in place. By insisting that whatever alternative plan the governors' committee proposed not involve deficit financing—that is, bonds—Weeks was sending a clear message to the states, namely that it was a settled issue that the federal government would raise user taxes; the only question now was which taxes and by how much.

Next to speak was Secretary Humphrey, who finally said out loud what he had clearly been thinking about the Clay plan's funding proposal all along: "Sec. Humphrey stated . . . his strong feeling that he had made a mistake in testifying for the [Clay plan's] bond proposal in the program last year." Having been dragooned into supporting the Clay proposal until its bitter end, Humphrey was now at liberty to throw his support behind an alternative that actually stood a chance of gaining bipartisan support in Congress: "He now recognized that Congress could not be committed for future years to agreement that certain taxes should be levied for certain purposes, hence the proposed bonds [under the Clay plan] would have been backed only by the good faith of the Government and general revenues." For Humphrey to be this candid about his previous public statements in support of the Clay plan, it no doubt helped that neither Eisenhower nor Clay, the mastermind of the discredited government corporation bond proposal, was present at this cabinet meeting. Accordingly, discussion of the highway program at the October 28 cabinet meeting ended with "general agreement to [the Weeks Committee's proposal] for presentation to the Governors during the coming week."

On November 3, Secretary Weeks met with the newly appointed governors' committee on highways. Also in attendance was Dan Throop Smith, a prominent economist then working for the Treasury Department; Smith was presumably filling in for Secretary Humphrey. The following day, Smith sent Humphrey a memorandum of the meeting, which begins: "The Governors' reaction to the proposal for a pay-as-we-go highway program was not good."[18] There were two main objections shared by those on the governors' committee who disliked the Weeks proposal. Some governors felt that the states could complete a better highway program without the aid of the federal government if they were able to increase gas taxes themselves; federal taxes would deprive the states of the resources they would need to build their own highways. Second, some states already had their own toll roads, and a new federal interstate system would deprive those states of tolls they would otherwise receive from these previously constructed roads.

These objections were a nonstarter because they presupposed a legislative possibility that was already off the table for the Weeks Committee, namely that the federal government would simply defer to the states and that there would be no federal interstate system whatsoever. Because the Weeks Committee was already committed to a single federal system, the question that *was* still on the table chiefly concerned how that system would be funded. This is the question Weeks turned to after hearing the governors' objections.

Weeks outlined the alternative funding mechanism: "(1) the Clay program, (2) additional taxes, (3) taxes and some temporary borrowing, (4) deficit financing, and (5) toll roads." He then used process of elimination to justify the new committee's plan: "The Clay proposal was not acceptable to Congress," and "no one seemed to want the Federal government to use toll roads." Finally, everyone knew the president would veto a bill that proposed deficit financing. This left raising taxes, with the possibility of temporary borrowing to make up any unforeseen shortages in future tax revenue. Though the governors appear to have been less than supportive of the tax increases, they also appear not to have resisted the Weeks plan with much energy besides demanding that states be compensated for previously constructed toll roads (a plan that, as Smith observes, had been part of the Clay proposal). Acquiescing to a rise in gas taxes, the governors also urged Weeks to raise taxes on truckers, a feat that, according to Governor Frank Lausche of Ohio, "the states had been unsuccessful [at]," likely because of the strength of the trucking lobby vis-à-vis state legislatures.

In the weeks following the meeting with the governors' committee, Secretary Humphrey continued to lobby for accommodating congressional Democrats and against retaining the Clay proposal.[19] His efforts paid off. Eisenhower's January 5, 1956, Annual Message to Congress—read to a joint session of Congress by a House clerk because the president was still recovering—did not explicitly embrace the Democratic plan or indicate that his administration was working on a new plan of its own. Yet it did express new openness to a range of possible funding plans. (It also made no mention of the Clay plan, thereby implicitly conceding its defeat.) Specifically, Eisenhower states that "the pressing nature of this problem must not lead us to solutions outside the bounds of sound fiscal management. As in the case of other pressing problems, there must be an adequate plan for financing."[20] In addition to this open-ended and noncommittal statement, Ike made explicit one point he had previously left vague: "The whole interstate system must be authorized as one project." With this assertion, Eisenhower jettisoned his previous professions of commitment to a cooperating federal/state/county arrangement. He had finally come down on the side of central planning, funding, and execution.

Humphrey continued to press his advantage in the weeks that followed. At the January 31 legislative conference, Staff Secretary Minnich notes in a memorandum to Budget Director Hughes, "It was agreed that in order to increase the chance of success of [the interstate highway] program the Administration should yield to Democratic insistence on financing through new or additional taxes and should cooperate in the development of an appropriate tax proposal to finance construction without any resort to deficit spending or dependence on existing revenues."[21] Administration officials and congressional Republicans had finally conceded what had been obvious since the Senate's passage of the Gore bill—indeed, since Finance Chairman Byrd's excoriation of the Clay bill in late 1954 and early 1955. To this end, "it was suggested that the Chairman of the Senate Finance Committee"—Senator Byrd—"be consulted as to the most desirable procedures for expediting completion of action on the bill."

No doubt with Byrd's fiscal principles in mind, on February 8, Secretary Humphrey drafted his idea for what would become the most important and innovative feature of the Federal Highway Act: the Highway Trust Fund. Aware of previous debates over how user taxes would be allocated toward highway construction, and whether funds from general tax revenue would be used for construction in the case of shortages in user revenue, Humphrey proposed creating a special account in the US

Treasury for highway tax revenue, an account explicitly modeled after the Social Security Fund, which had been created in 1935 ("the Federal Old-Age and Survivors Insurance trust fund").[22] In short, the equivalent amount of all revenue from the proposed bill's raised user taxes (on gasoline, tires, etc.) would be deposited in a special account or "trust fund" at the end of each fiscal year; these funds would be used to meet all expenditures for highway construction. In addition, the act would authorize the treasury secretary to advance general US Treasury funds "not otherwise appropriated" to the Highway Trust Fund in case the fund failed to meet expenses in a given year, "provided, that the general fund appropriation shall be reimbursed in the amount of such advances from time to time as moneys become available in the fund from subsequent appropriations of the additional [highway user] taxes."[23]

Hail, Boggs! Fallon–Boggs and the Highway Trust Fund

With the Eisenhower administration relenting on the Clay proposal, House Democrats finally had enough time and mutual cooperation to draft a highway bill that would win over, rather than alienate, its most interested constituencies. No longer under the gun to pass a bill in a severely constrained time frame, the House began considering a new highway bill in early February 1956 giving them more than seven months to hold hearings and write a bill that gained necessary consent. The process started with Representative Hale Boggs, Democrat from Louisiana and a member of the Ways and Means Committee. On February 6, notes a *New York Times* report, Boggs "introduced a bill designed to raise such additional levies [of $36.5 billion in highway user tax revenue]. The measure had the blessings of Sam Rayburn, Speaker of the House, and Representative Joel Cooper, Democrat of Tennessee and chairman of the Ways and Means Committee."[24] The *Times* article also notes that "President Eisenhower, previously supporting bond issues [sic] financing, has joined the user-tax movement."

In turn, Boggs solicited input from Secretary Humphrey, by now recognized as one of the leading proponents of a compromise highway plan in the Eisenhower administration, and an open supporter of a highway bill that resembled the Fallon bill. Originally, Boggs had considered only a "rough linkage between highway user tax revenue and highway funding."[25] But during testimony before the Ways and Means Committee on February 14, Humphrey pointed out that the revenue bill currently being considered by Ways and Means would leave a deficit because it would not be able to pay for the Fallon bill's construction projects.

> Mr. Boggs: Do you think the proposals before the committee in the bill are fair?
>
> Secretary Humphrey: They will not raise the money. The trouble with the bill is that it leaves a great big deficit.[26]

Boggs followed this exchange up by asking how Humphrey would propose closing the revenue gap in question. Humphrey responds that he does not wish to say how the tax burden should be imposed on specific highway users and highway adjacent manufacturers: "I am not to judge that, Mr. Boggs. That is your job. Your function is to decide how you levy the tax. . . . Who is the proper fellow to put the burden on?"[27] As for how to structure the revenue and expenditures, however, Humphrey goes on to state that he has "made a complete recommendation as to how you can proceed." At this point, questioning is taken over by Representative John Byrnes, a Republican from Wisconsin, who asks Humphrey how highway user tax revenue would "not in the future get mingled up with general fund operations," so that Congress would "know where we are going as far as actual revenues for road purposes [are concerned]?" In response, Humphrey lays out the plan he sketched in the draft bill from February 8:

> I would suggest this, Mr. Byrnes, that we follow a practice similar to the practice that is followed for the social security and the other funds, and that we do not get to the physical earmarking of funds, but that we do as we do with those funds; that we estimate the amounts to be collected in these categories, and that those amounts be deposited in a special fund to the credit of a special fund; that the withdrawals then be made from that fund; that credits in that fund shall not be credits to the budget; but that deficits in that fund shall be deficits in the budget.[28]

One of the chief advantages of the trust fund system was that it would be able to capitalize on tax revenue that would invariably increase as the number of cars and trucks using the expanded highways increased. Generally speaking, the logic of the trust fund was that ever-more highways could be built in the future because more and better highways enable and incentivize more highway users. In turn, these users necessitate more fuel, tires, and car and truck construction, all of which pay taxes that are funneled into the Highway Trust Fund. This is the point that Chairman Jere Cooper makes near the end of Humphrey's testimony: "In making these estimates of the amount of revenue to be produced from these various types of commodities that are used in highway use, do you take into account the very probable increase in the use of these commodities on the highways with a better highway system?"[29]

Finally, in one of the most revealing moments of his participation in the broader cause of interstate highway reform, Humphrey publicly and unequivocally rejected the Clay plan. Asked by Representative Frank Karsten (D-MO) if there was a reason why he had not been referring to his above described plan as the "President's proposal," Humphrey pulled no punches.

> Secretary Humphrey: Yes, Mr. Karsten. As I understand it, the President's program is dead. That met with disapproval, such general disapproval, at the last session of the Congress, that as far as I know it is completely forgotten, and we are on an entirely new tack, here.
>
> Mr. Karsten: Well, this is a program different from the President's program. Is that correct?
>
> Secretary Humphrey: Yes, it is.
>
> Mr. Karsten: It is not clear to me whether you are appearing in support of this program or just as an expert witness. Would you enlighten me as to whether you are in favor of it or you are opposed to it.
>
> Secretary Humphrey: I am in favor of the program that is being discussed, which is a pay-as-you-build program.

Mr. Karsten: Do you think it is as good as the program that you proposed last year?

Secretary Humphrey: I think it is better, personally.

As a consequence of Humphrey's testimony, "the next version of the [highway] bill proposed a Highway Trust Fund—a crediting mechanism for keeping track of highway user tax revenue."[30]

As they would have done in 1955 had they been permitted to write the highway bill's revenue package, the Ways and Means Committee held a total of six days' worth of hearings, starting February 14 and ending February 21. The hearings canvassed highway experts and, importantly, representatives of users who would bear the new program's tax burden. This time around, the bill was received encouragingly by its most important constituents. "In the trucking industry," writes Rose, "men talked of concessions. Between February and April 1956, in meetings, in industry-wide publications, and in correspondence with members of Congress, they announced again their willingness to pay higher taxes. . . . Beginning as early as February, then, once rates were fixed, truckers urged House members to vote for the Boggs-Fallon bill."[31]

Ways and Means reported out Boggs's revenue bill on March 19, and it was sent to the Public Works Committee, where it and the Fallon bill were integrated into a complete highway program. Public Works approved the whole program on April 21, and it was scheduled for a vote on April 27. At a news conference on April 25, a few days after the House scheduled its floor vote, Eisenhower was asked about the "revised highway bill" that was about to be taken up by the House.[32] Characteristically, Ike did not endorse the bill, instead remarking: "We need highways badly, very badly, and I am in favor of any forward, constructive step in this field." To date, this was probably the president's most supportive comment on the Democratic highway program.

On April 27, with more than two months to go before the summer recess, the House passed Boggs–Fallon by an overwhelming 388–19 vote. Unlike the Fallon bill of 1955, which raised user taxes without their consent and proposed an unwieldly revenue package without the input of the House's main revenue authority, Ways and Means, Fallon–Boggs was popular because it "incorporated long-sought goals, asked few significant sacrifices, and managed to sidestep difficult questions."[33] Indeed, "Boggs and Fallon had found the key to success. They promised plenty of new roadway for everyone and security for treasury deposits, and had asked truckers to pay only modest tax increases."[34]

Because the Senate had already passed a highway bill the previous spring, significantly less legwork was needed to reach an agreement about the bill; the House and Senate were able to proceed directly to conference committee without the Senate having to take another vote. Conference committee negotiations went relatively easily because the most controversial element of the program—the revenue proposal—had been resolved in the House, and the Gore bill had been silent as to taxes and funding. The Senate simply filled in the Gore bill with the funding program in Boggs-Fallon, and worked out additional differences regarding the actual highway plan, including questions about routes and apportionment of funding.

The conference committee reported its final bill out on June 25, and the House and Senate voted the following day. The Senate approved the bill 89-1, and the House approved it without a roll call, signaling its overwhelming popularity. On June 29, Eisenhower, again ill, signed the 1956 Federal-Aid and Defense Highway Act into law from his hospital bed at the Walter Reed Medical Center.

CONCLUSION

The chief purpose of this book has been to pinpoint and clarify the most important decisions Dwight Eisenhower made in his effort to advance federal highway legislation, and to give a sense of the role those decisions played in effecting that landmark policy change. Eisenhower's role was ambiguous at best. Inherited folk wisdom about his leadership—fortified by generations of scholars and biographers—must be revised in light of other, less familiar considerations, including the role of congressional Democrats and the failure of the President's Advisory Committee (PAC) led by General Lucius Clay. As a consequence, although my discussion of Eisenhower's actions during 1952–1956 is certainly relevant to anyone interested in exploring questions of causality—why did Eisenhower succeed and fail where he did?—it is not meant to meet that burden itself. An adequate account of the reasons for successful passage of the 1956 highway bill would need to canvas and analyze a range of considerations well beyond the scope of this book, which is primarily a discussion of the decisions of one man. That being said, let me add a few words in the remaining pages about the significance and relevance of Eisenhower's role in federal highway expansion for some of the major alternative theories of the presidency within political science. What does the story of Eisenhower's role in federal highway expansion tell us about presidential leadership, presidential management, and the institutions of the presidency and the broader executive branch?

Several generations of scholars from different backgrounds have speculated about the sources and causes of presidential failure—that is, why presidents succeed in realizing their goals in some cases and fail in others. As these scholars have shown, answering this question requires addressing and clarifying a number of ancillary puzzles. Given that victories are often delayed and diluted, what does it mean for a president to succeed in the first place? How can we accurately gauge the extent of a president's agency in a given policy change? And are the conditions of presidential success rooted more in personal factors, such as the president's individual leadership abilities, or in structural factors, such as the features of the office a given president inherits?

Among a handful of major themes, this book has focused on the challenges Eisenhower faced in trying to pass his preferred highway program, one that would have neither raised taxes nor added to the national debt. Scholars of the presidency will be led to wonder about the sources of these challenges. Were they consequences of Ike's own leadership style, such that a different, more skillful leader might have devised ways to overcome them? Or were they rooted in structural factors that were simply beyond his control?

In regard to Eisenhower's personal leadership style, scholars going back to Richard Neustadt have observed striking differences between Ike and his immediate predecessors, Franklin Roosevelt and Harry Truman.[1] These presidents had been unafraid to use informal negotiations and partisan politicking to achieve their leadership ends—indeed, each seemed to appreciate the extent to which such means were core rather than peripheral elements to the job of modern presidential governance. In his landmark *Hidden-Hand Presidency*, Fred Greenstein went some distance in correcting the exaggerated view that Eisenhower was simply anathema to the Roosevelt leadership model, showing that part of Ike's skill as an effective leader consisted in his ability to disguise active interventions in the policymaking process behind a façade of benign, Olympian reserve.[2] And yet, as I have tried to suggest in these pages, there is a sense in which the older, pre-Greenstein wisdom captures the essential character of Eisenhower's approach to the presidency. And though it is true that Eisenhower had strong policy preferences, and that—notwithstanding his statesmanlike affectations—he was by no means disengaged from the minutia of the legislative process, his role in federal highway reform exhibited some personality traits that appear likely to have handicapped his ability to negotiate politically in a way that would have brought him closer to his preferred policy outcome. Using Erwin Hargrove's approach, it is helpful to interpret Eisenhower as a politically talented individual who, nevertheless, suffered from tendencies that persisted in hindering his political goals because they were central features of—and therefore not easily divorceable from—who he was as a human being.[3]

One such tendency was Eisenhower's unshakable confidence in his own integrity and uprightness. As scholars have observed, and as I have tried to document, Eisenhower disliked adversarial negotiations of any kind. Part of that aversion seems to have been rooted in his belief that his personal incorruptibility should have largely eliminated the need for negotiations in the first place. During discussions over highway expansion, for example, he was inclined to see bad faith and "low" partisanship motivating those who disagreed with him. At the same time, he was entirely unable to appreciate why his own actions—for example, appointing members of his "gang" of millionaire friends to prominent administrative positions, or refusing (again and again) to admit that the Clay proposal would have added to the national debt—might have appeared less than admirable to others. He tended to shut down when he felt that the purity of his motivations was being doubted or dismissed, as he did during his February 16, 1955, meeting with congressional Democrats.

These qualities made him admirable in the eyes of many, but they undermined his ability to assemble a coalition in favor of highway expansion because they led him to dismiss out of hand anyone who dared to question whether the Clay plan—which he came to view as *his* plan—actually adhered to the governmental principles that he, Eisenhower, espoused. In some ways, Ike's self-confidence—which is a necessary trait in leaders—hindered his capacity for empathy, and prevented him from understanding why his own uprightness was less obvious to other people than it was to himself. (In doodles drawn during political meetings, Eisenhower sometimes depicted himself as a heroic figure leading others—perhaps thereby gratifying a disappointed desire to receive unconditional deference from those whom in real life he viewed as properly subordinates.[4]) In the case of highway reform, at least, these qualities rendered him inflexible and caused him to alienate many of the allies—Democratic and Republican—he would have needed to build an idiosyncratic majority. As a consequence, that task was left to congressional Democrats more adept at the kind of logrolling that struck Eisenhower as loathsome, including George Fallon, Albert Gore Sr., Dennis Chavez, and Hale Boggs.

From a more structural perspective, we can conceive of the difficulties Eisenhower met with as rooted in contradictions that are unintended design features of the presidential office he inhabited, the office of the "modern presidency." For despite being characterized as a "Whig" president who as such tended to leave the task of legislating to Congress, Ike inhabited a presidential office that had been forged, not by William Henry Harrison and Millard Fillmore, but by Franklin Roosevelt.[5] And as Andrew Rudalevige has suggested, modern presidents in the latter tradition have the option to centralize the policymaking process within the White House, in order to try to control the procedures and outcomes of the legislative process. But centralization entails difficulties of its own, and there is no guarantee that greater centralization will increase the odds of success.[6] Seen from this vantage point, Eisenhower pursued a legislative strategy that was in many ways self-defeating because he was in the grips of institutional and ideational forces that were the inheritance of past reforms and that were largely beyond his control. Specifically, he developed a comprehensive highway program within his own White House without any congressional involvement—Republican or Democratic—before presenting his plan to Congress on a take-it-or-leave-it basis. He defended his decision to sideline Congress on the grounds that he was complying with the legal-constitutional doctrine of separation of powers. For Eisenhower, this imperative meant that presidents should refrain from negotiating with members of Congress to secure passage of their preferred legislation, because such negotiations would violate the "mutual independence" of legislative and executive power as embodied in Congress and the presidency. Instead, he held that it was the president who should actually write legislation, and that Congress should simply approve or reject the president's proposals without contributing substantively.[7] Accordingly, Ike claimed to have offered himself "as a political leader to unseat the New Deal–Fair Deal bureaucracy in Washington" on the grounds that his predecessors had farmed out the job of legislating to bureaucrats who had eclipsed Congress.[8] Yet once in power, and despite indications what he would pursue a different style of policymaking, he did not systematically return power to Congress, but instead assigned the tasks previously performed by bureaucrats and policy experts to business and industry leaders from the private sector. In the case of highway legislation, Eisenhower justified sidelining Congress and retaining control of bill-writing by questioning "the ability of a free government to continue functioning in spite of pressures from groups inside the body politic, where these pressures are created by immediate self-interest."[9]

Along these lines, scholars who have delineated the complexities and pitfalls of the modern presidency might conclude that Eisenhower was responding to the incentive structure of a presidential office that had been reconstructed by early twentieth-century reformers to remedy alleged defects in the design of the US Constitution.[10] Advocates for a characteristically "modern" presidency rejected the practice of their nineteenth-century predecessors on the grounds that letting Congress and congressional party organizations take the initiative in legislating involved too many special interests, and resulted in a government that was broadly unresponsive to urgent societal problems.[11] Nineteenth-century norms had counseled presidents to present Congress with a set of broad policy principles rather than a completed bill, and to allow legislators time and space to deliberate on those principles and to negotiate over their own preferences. Accordingly, what distinguishes modern presidents from their predecessors is neither legislative ambition nor their willingness to negotiate informally with members of Congress—nineteenth-century presidents did both of these.[12] Rather, it is their inclination to develop complete domestic policy programs behind closed doors by means of expert administrators, or private-sector officials, or both—proposals they then present to Congress as finished products to be voted up or down but not substantively altered.[13] Developmentally, these institutional changes have resulted in episodic migrations of legislative authority from the Congress to the presidency.[14] Under this new conception of constitutional authority, which has spawned vocal normative defenders, Congress does not—or at least should not—contribute to the substance of legislation.[15] Rather, it should serve as a kind of rubber stamp to approve or reject the president's bills.

Perversely, Eisenhower complied with this presidential incentive structure in ways that had the effect of undermining his ability to realize the aspiration of the modern presidency: passing his preferred highway program with minimal congressional interference. Indeed, far from embodying a "Whig" ethos, as some scholars have suggested, Ike farmed out the job of designing a highway bill to officials within his White House and to interested members of the private sector in the hopes of avoiding negotiations with members of Congress.[16] Yet these machinations had the very opposite effect of those he intended. They imported into the White House the very same negotiations, turf wars, and factional conflicts Eisenhower had tried to avoid by sidelining Congress in the first place, thereby doubling the number of obstacles that stood in the way of passing a highway bill: whatever highway plan his administration negotiated among themselves would have to be renegotiated in Congress, unless the president was able to secure congressional approval of his completed plan (he was not). In addition, Ike's White House was ill-equipped to handle the legislative hurly-burly of logrolling and horse trading. In the end, his highway team became a miniature Congress whose infighting and dysfunction undermined the very goals Eisenhower had tried to pursue by circumventing the actual Congress in the first place.

NOTES

INTRODUCTION: PRESIDENTIAL DECISIONS

1. Dwight D. Eisenhower, *The Papers of Dwight David Eisenhower*, vol. 16, pt. 7, chap. 15 (Baltimore: Johns Hopkins University Press, 1971), 1691. Hereafter *Eisenhower Papers*.

2. For Eisenhower's smoking habits, see Dwight D. Eisenhower, *At Ease: Stories I Tell Friends* (New York: Eastern Acorn Press, 1981), 354.

3. Quoted in Richard Weingroff, "The Man Who Changed America, Part I," *Public Roads* 66, no. 5 (2003).

4. For contrasting views of what matters presidents are able to decide for themselves, see Richard Neustadt, *Presidential Power* (New York: The Free Press, 1990), chap. 2; William Howell, *Power without Persuasion* (Princeton, NJ: Princeton University Press, 2003); Herbert J. Storing, *Toward a More Perfect Union*, ed. Joseph M. Bessette (Washington, DC: AEI Press, 1997), chaps. 18–20; Joseph M. Bessette and Jeffrey K. Tulis, "The Constitution, Politics, and the Presidency," in *The Presidency in the Constitutional Order*, ed. Bessette and Tulis (New York: Routledge, 2010), 3–30.

5. See, for example, Stephen Ambrose, *Eisenhower*, Vol. 2, *The President* (New York: Simon and Schuster, 1984), 250; Peter Norton, "Be Like Ike," The Miller Center Series on Issues & Policy, January 10, 2017, https://millercenter.org/issues-policy/economics/be-like-ike.

6. This would be especially strange, since serious work on the German *Autobahn* did not begin until the Nazi period. Eisenhower admired German highways, not because of some fascination with Germany, but because the German example seemed to illustrate a generally applicable principle, namely, that federal action in the area of transportation can contribute to the general welfare of *any* country in politically and economic tangible ways.

7. See the Department of Transportation's website, https://www.fhwa.dot.gov/programadmin/interstate.cfm.

8. The earliest and in some ways most comprehensive of these works is Mark Rose, *Interstate: Express Highway Politics, 1939–1989* (Knoxville: University of Tennessee Press, 1990). Also invaluable are Tom Lewis, *Divided Highways* (Ithaca, NY: Cornell University Press, 2013), and the research of Jeff Davis at the Eno Center for Transportation and Richard Weingroff at the Department of Transportation.

9. Ambrose, *Eisenhower*, 2:251.

10. Ambrose seems to have hastily skimmed Mark Rose's account of these developments; see Ambrose, *Eisenhower*, 2:692n67. The problem is that Rose clearly provides the information Ambrose gets wrong; see Rose, *Interstate*, 81, 82.

11. Jean Edward Smith, *Eisenhower in War and Peace* (New York: Random House, 2013), 651.

12. Unsurprisingly, advocates of governmental activism, including Woodrow

Wilson, FDR, and Truman, had all supported dramatic highway expansion; as I will discuss in chapter 2, all met with a few limited successes and numerous failures.

13. For a comprehensive treatment of this struggle, see Rose, *Interstate*, chap. 1, and Federal Highway Administration, *America's Highways, 1776–1976* (Washington, DC: US Government Printing Office, 1976), chaps. 6–12.

14. For a particularly illuminating overview of Johnson's style of leadership, see Jeffrey K. Tulis, *The Rhetorical Presidency* (Princeton, NJ: Princeton University Press, 2017), 161–172.

15. See Ambrose, *Eisenhower*, 2:218.

16. Fred I. Greenstein, *The Hidden-Hand Presidency*, 2nd ed. (Baltimore: Johns Hopkins University Press, 1994).

17. Stephen Hess, "What Congress Looked Like from Inside the Eisenhower White House," Brookings, January 6, 2012, https://www.brookings.edu/research/what-congress-looked-like-from-inside-the-eisenhower-white-house/. See also Smith, *Eisenhower*, xiv: "Eisenhower held a textbook view of presidential power. As more than one scholar has observed, he may have been the last president to actually believe in the Constitution. For Ike, Congress made policy and the president carried it out."

18. I discuss the idea of the "modern presidency," and the implications of my argument about Eisenhower for that idea, in the conclusion of this book.

CHAPTER 1. BACKGROUND AND CONTEXT, 1787–1952

1. US Department of Transportation (DOT), *America's Highways 1776–1976* (Washington, DC: Government Printing Office, 1976), 88; Stephen Skowronek, *Building a New American State* (New York: Cambridge University Press, 1982), 19–35. This is not to say that the early US states were entirely lacking in ambition; see, for example, Charles U. Zug, "Nationalization and State Building in the Early American Republic: The Act for the Relief of Sick and Disabled Seamen," *Journal of Law and Courts* 9, no. 2 (2021): 283–302; Jeffrey K. Tulis and Nicole Mellow, *Legacies of Losing in American Politics* (Chicago: University of Chicago Press, 2018), chap. 2.

2. DOT, *America's Highways*, 6.

3. DOT, 8.

4. Stephen Minicucci, "Internal Improvements and the Union, 1790–1860," *Studies in American Political Development* 18 (Fall 2004): 160–185.

5. DOT, *America's Highways*, 11.

6. DOT, 13.

7. DOT, 14, 29.

8. DOT, 41.

9. DOT, 80–87.

10. DOT, 86–87.

11. DOT, 176.

12. DOT, 177–179.
13. Rose, *Interstate*, 19.
14. Rose, 27.
15. Rose, 23.
16. Some scholars have suggested that this experience engendered in Eisenhower a lifelong concern with roadbuilding, which culminated in his support for highway expansion during his first term as president. However, there is little evidence in his public and private utterances from 1919 to 1952 to suggest that he was any more concerned with highways than any other public-spirited American would have been. See Eisenhower, *At Ease*, 157–166.
17. E.g., Ambrose, *Eisenhower*, 1:206–207.
18. Dwight D. Eisenhower, "State of the Union Address—1953." See also Ambrose, *Eisenhower*, 1:509.
19. Ambrose, *Eisenhower*, 2:39.
20. Ambrose, *Eisenhower*, 2:48; *Eisenhower*, 1:512; Eisenhower, diary entry from February 9, 1953, in Dwight D. Eisenhower, *The Eisenhower Diaries*, ed. Robert Ferrell (New York: Norton, 1981), 228.
21. Ambrose, *Eisenhower*, 2:99, 69.
22. E.g., Ambrose, *Eisenhower*, 1:553, 568–570.
23. *Congressional Record*, House, February 22, 1955, 1904.
24. See Ambrose, *Eisenhower*, 1:510–12, 525.
25. In his diary, Eisenhower described himself as having offered himself "as a political leader to unseat the New Deal-Fair Deal bureaucracy" (see *Eisenhower Diaries*, 231).
26. Ambrose, *Eisenhower*, 1:511.
27. Ambrose, *Eisenhower*, 1:490–491.
28. Ambrose, *Eisenhower*, 1:476; *Eisenhower*, 2:28.
29. Michael Beschloss, "The Gang That Always Liked Ike," *New York Times*, November 15, 2014.
30. Ambrose, *Eisenhower*, 2:73.
31. See Ambrose, *Eisenhower*, 2:26–27, 96, 94. See also Beschloss, "The Gang": "Some members of the Gang and other friends gave [Eisenhower] gifts, such as cattle for his Gettysburg farm. They also helped finance his Augusta golf cottage—called 'Mamie's Cabin,' in the first lady's honor."
32. Ambrose, *Eisenhower*, 1:476.
33. Ambrose, *Eisenhower*, 2:28.
34. Beschloss, "The Gang."
35. "Washington Wire," *The New Republic*, December 15, 1952. The plumber in question was Martin Durkin, head of the AFL plumbers union; see Ambrose, *Eisenhower*, 2:24.
36. Beschloss, "The Gang." See also "The Eisenhower Cabinet," *The New Republic*, December 1, 1952.
37. Ambrose, *Eisenhower*, 2:20.
38. Eisenhower, *Eisenhower Diaries*, 226–227.

39. "The Eisenhower Cabinet," *The New Republic*, December 1, 1952.
40. Dwight D. Eisenhower, *Mandate for Change* (New York: Doubleday, 1963), 271.
41. Beschloss, "The Gang."
42. Ambrose, *Eisenhower*, 2:27.

CHAPTER 2. PRESIDENTIAL INITIATIVE: EISENHOWER'S INITIAL FORAYS INTO HIGHWAY EXPANSION, 1952–1954

1. *Eisenhower Papers*, vol. 14, pt. 1, chap. 1, 33.
2. Dwight D. Eisenhower, "Annual Message to the Congress on the State of the Union," February 2, 1953, American Presidency Project, https://www.presidency.ucsb.edu/node/231684.
3. See "Ike Understands Road Problem We're Facing," *Road Builders' News* 29, nos. 11–12 (1952): 7.
4. Memorandum to Gabriel Hague from Eisenhower, February 4, 1953, in *Eisenhower Papers* vol. 14, pt. 1, chap. 1, 23–25.
5. In 1940, Buckner, a graduate of Harvard Law School, married Helen Watson, a New York philanthropist and daughter of the president of IBM, Thomas J. Watson. Helen was a debutante at the Royal Court in London; see *New York Times*, July 2, 1940, 24. According to a 1956 campaign finance report by the Senate, Buckner donated $2,000 to the Republican Party in the 1956 general election, equivalent to $20,860 in 2022 dollars; see "1956 General Election Campaigns: Report of the Subcommittee on Privileges and Elections" (Washington, DC: US Government Printing Office, 1957), exhibit 27, 114.
6. *Eisenhower Papers*, vol. 14, pt. 1, chap. 1, 25n2.
7. "Survey of Some Potential Self-Liquidating Projects," Walker G. Buckner, February 4, 1953 (DDEL: Ann Whitman File, Name Series, Box 3, folder "Buckner, Walter Gentry"), 1. DDEL = Dwight David Eisenhower Library.
8. Robert A. Bennett, "Gabriel Hauge, Banker, Dies," *New York Times*, July 25, 1981.
9. Memorandum from DDE to Gabriel Hauge, in *Eisenhower Papers*, vol. 14, pt. 1, chap. 1, 24.
10. DDE to Hauge, 24.
11. See https://www.archives.gov/research/guide-fed-records/groups/030.html.
12. Lewis, *Divided Highways*, 100.
13. Memorandum from DDE to Dodge, November 5, 1953 (Eisenhower Library).
14. DDE to Dodge, 1.
15. DDE to Dodge, 1 (underline in original).
16. Eisenhower, "Annual Message to the Congress on the State of the Union," January 7, 1954, American Presidency Project, https://www.presidency.ucsb.edu/documents/annual-message-the-congress-the-state-the-union-13.
17. DDE to Burns, in *Eisenhower Papers*, vol. 15, pt. 4, chap. 9, 867–869.

18. DDE to Burns, 868.
19. Handwritten notes of Cabinet Meeting, February 5, 1954 (Hagerty Diary: Eisenhower Library).
20. February 5, 1954, Cabinet Meeting, 1.
21. February 5, 1954, Cabinet Meeting, 2.
22. Rose, *Interstate*, 70.
23. Murray to Hauge, December 23, 1953 (WHCF/OF, 122); see *Eisenhower Papers*, vol. 14, pt. 1, chap. 1, 25n4.
24. Lewis, *Divided Highways*, 101.
25. Notes of conference with J. S. Bragdon and Robert Murray, April 9, 1954 (DDEL: Bragdon Files).
26. According to Bragdon, Murray concluded his remarks about highway policy by stating that "he would welcome a supplemental program of any size."
27. Memorandum of "Conference in the White House," April 12, 1954 (DDEL: Bragdon Files).
28. See Rose, *Interstate*, 71n2. See also Lewis, *Divided Highways*, 101.
29. Rose, *Interstate*, 71.
30. Memorandum of conversation between J. S. Bragdon and Francis du Pont, April 12, 1954 (Bragdon Records, Box 37, folder "Highways—1954 [April—August]," Eisenhower Library).
31. Bragdon–Du Pont memorandum, 1.
32. Bragdon–Du Pont memorandum, 1.
33. "Notes on Draft for National Highway Defense Bill," April 16, 1954 (DDEL: Bragdon Files).
34. See J. S. Bragdon Office Memorandum of April 12, 1954 (DDEL: Bragdon Files); Memorandum from Bragdon to Buckner, April 21, 1954 (DDEL: Bragdon Files).
35. Rose, *Interstate*, 71.
36. Bragdon to Buckner, April 21, 1954, 2.
37. Bragdon to Buckner, 3.
38. Rose, *Interstate*, 71.
39. Lewis, *Divided Highways*, 101.
40. Draft of Bill for Highway Legislation by Tallamy and Moses, May 4, 1954 (DDEL).
41. Memorandum from Bertram Tallamy and Robert Moses to Sherman Adams, May 4, 1954 (DDEL).
42. Message from DDE to Sherman Adams, May 11, 1954, in *Eisenhower Papers*, vol. 15, pt. 5, chap. 10, 1067.
43. Rose, *Interstate*, 72.
44. Rose, 72.
45. Rose, 72.
46. Bragdon's office produced a sixth draft dated "6/1/54." See "An Act," June 1, 1954 (DDEL: Bragdon Files, Box 59).
47. Sherman Adams, *Firsthand Report* (New York: Harper & Brothers, 1961).

CHAPTER 3. THE CLAY COMMITTEE AND THE DEVELOPMENT OF EISENHOWER'S HIGHWAY PROGRAM, 1954-1955

1. Ambrose neglects to mention the death and asserts that Eisenhower sent Nixon in order to "build him up" as a potential successor in the 1956 presidential election (see Ambrose, *Eisenhower*, 2:251.

2. Richard Nixon, "Address of Vice President Richard Nixon to the Governors' Conference Lake George, New York, July 12, 1954," US Department of Transportation: Federal Highway Administration , Highway History, https://www.fhwa.dot.gov/infrastructure/rw96m.cfm. Hereafter cited as "Nixon Address."

3. See the CPI Inflation Calculator, https://www.in2013dollars.com/us/inflation/1954?amount=50000000000.

4. See Eisenhower, "Annual Budget Message to Congress: Fiscal Year 1955," 1954, American Presidency Project. https://www.presidency.ucsb.edu/documents/annual-budget-message-the-congress-fiscal-year-1955.

5. "Nixon Address," 2.

6. "Nixon Address," 4.

7. "Nixon Address," 2.

8. Gary Schwartz wonders about this same question, and based on interviews with BPR engineer Frank Turner (discussed in chapter 5) entertains the following explanation: "How Eisenhower was persuaded to accept the views expressed in the [July 12] address remains somewhat unclear. One possible explanation concerns Francis du Pont. . . . During the 1920s, du Pont's father had constructed a 5-mile route, which many regarded as the country's first superhighway, on land he owned in Delaware. . . . For the du Pont family, the promotion of superhighways became an idealistic mission. Within the Administration, du Pont apparently exerted a large influence on Eisenhower, who tended to be impressed by blue-ribbon businessmen of the du Pont sort"; see Schwartz, "Urban Freeways and the Interstate System," *Transportation Law Journal* 8 (1976): 187n156.

9. Helpful examples of this kind of presidential rhetoric include Theodore Roosevelt's campaign for expanded federal railroad regulation and Ronald Reagan's campaign for tax reform; see Tulis, *Rhetorical Presidency*, chaps. 4 and 7.

10. Sherman Adams outlines the resolution in his memorandum to the president. See below.

11. Eisenhower, "The President's News Conference," July 14, 1954, American Presidency Project, https://www.presidency.ucsb.edu/documents/the-presidents-news-conference-458.

12. Sherman Adams, "Memorandum for the President: Status of the National Highway Program," July 22, 1954 (DDEL: Bragdon Files).

13. Adams, "Status of National Highway Program," 2.

14. Adams, 1-2.

15. This seems to be incompatible with Weingroff's characterization of the process by which the PAC was formed; see Richard Weingroff, "General Lucius

D. Clay—The President's Man," Highway History, https://www.fhwa.dot.gov/in frastructure/clay.cfm. According to Weingroff, "When Sherman Adams . . . asked who should serve on the committee, the president said, 'Call General Clay.'" Eisenhower appears not to have settled on Clay until late August after having asked several other national business leaders to chair the PAC.

16. According to Jeff Davis at the Eno Center, the summary was "presumably made by Bragdon (looks like his typewriter and style)" (email correspondence, March 24, 2022).

17. Adams, "Status of National Highway Program," 3.

18. That Adams made this assumption is suggested by his recommendation that the president form a group of congressional Republicans who could sponsor the legislation at the appropriate time. Were Adams contemplating possible Democratic victories in 1954, presumably he would have suggested that Eisenhower meet with all the relevant congressional leaders and committee chairs, not just with Republicans.

19. I was unable to obtain a transcript of the phone call. However, Kyes's telegram to Eisenhower from the following day (July 24) mentions their conversation from "Friday," July 23.

20. Telegram from Roger Kyes to Dwight Eisenhower, July 24, 1954 (DDEL/Eno Center).

21. For a brief overview of Bane's career, see https://www.ssa.gov/history/fbane.html.

22. Frank Bane, Memorandum to Sherman Adams, July 26, 1954 (DDEL/Eno Center).

23. Memorandum to Sherman Adams from Gabriel Hauge, July 26, 1954 (DDEL/Eno Center).

24. Memorandum from Charles F. Willis Jr. to Sherman Adams, July 27, 1954 (DDEL/Eno Center).

25. Memorandum from Charles F. Willis Jr. to Sherman Adams, July 27, 1954 (DDEL/Eno Center). Willis's note is a response to Hauge's emphatic recommendation of Kyes, which had been circulated the previous day.

26. For a description of Collyer, who had served as a special director of the War Production Board starting in 1945, see "John L. Collyer, Goodrich Head, Appointed Controller of Rubber," *New York Times*, March 22, 1945, 17.

27. Rose, *Interstate*, 74.

28. Rose, 74.

29. See Memorandums from Bragdon to Burns, August 3, August 3 (a more developed version of the previous memorandum), and August 6, 1954 (DDEL: Bragdon Files).

30. Bragdon to Burns, August 6, 1954.

31. Memorandum from Arthur Minnich to Thomas E. Stephens, August 23, 1954 (DDEL/Eno Center).

32. Memorandum from Lucius Clay to Eisenhower, August 30, 1954 (DDEL/Eno Center), 1.

33. Clay to Eisenhower, August 30, 1954, 1–2. See also Weingroff, "The President's Man," 3.

34. General Carroll to Sherman Adams, September 2, 1954 (DDEL/Eno Center).

35. Draft of Telegram from Gabriel Hauge to James Hagerty, September 3, 1954 (DDEL/Eno Center) (my emphasis).

36. Telegram from Gabriel Hauge to James Hagerty (attn. Wayne Hawks), September 3, 1954 (DDEL/Eno Center).

37. Quoted in Weingroff, "The President's Man," 3.

38. Hauge to Hagerty, September 3, 1954.

39. Eisenhower, *Mandate for Change*, 434.

40. Adams, *Firsthand Report*, 166: "As time ran out in October . . . Republican leaders who had worked with us in 1952 come with increasing frequency to my office in the White House with statistics from the pollsters showing that a Democratic victory was looming and the only way it could be prevented was by the president himself." See also Ambrose, *Eisenhower*, 2:218.

41. E.g., Eisenhower, *Mandate for Change*, 436.

42. Dwight D. Eisenhower, "Address at the Hollywood Bowl, Los Angeles, California," September 23, 1954, American Presidency Project, https://www.presidency.ucsb.edu/documents/address-the-hollywood-bowl-los-angeles-california.

43. D. B. Hardeman and Donald C. Bacon, *Rayburn: A Biography* (Austin: Texas Monthly Press, 1987), 385.

44. Adams, *Firsthand Report*, 166.

45. See Daniel Galvin, *Presidential Party Building* (Princeton, NJ: Princeton University Press, 2010), chap. 3.

46. Eisenhower, *Mandate for Change*, 459.

47. Eisenhower, "Hollywood Bowl."

48. Eisenhower made the same point about highways in similar versions of this stump speech given throughout his campaign; see "Address at the Republican Precinct Day Rally, Denver, CO," October 8, 1954, https://www.presidency.ucsb.edu/documents/address-the-republican-precinct-day-rally-denver-colorado; "Address at the Forrestal Memorial Award Dinner of the National Security Industrial Association," October 25, 1954, https://www.presidency.ucsb.edu/documents/address-the-forrestal-memorial-award-dinner-the-national-security-industrial-association; and "Remarks at New Castle County Airport, Wilmington, Delaware," October 29, 1954, https://www.presidency.ucsb.edu/documents/remarks-new-castle-county-airport-wilmington-delaware.

49. Rose, *Interstate*, 74.

50. Rose, 74.

51. Rose, 143n14.

52. Rose, 74.

53. Rose, 75.

54. Rose, 75.

55. Rose, 75: "General Clay . . . was virtually indifferent to proposals sent his way by the Treasury Department and Budget Bureau officials, producing a second rift within government circles."

56. Lewis, *Divided Highways*, 110.

57. Weingroff, "The President's Man," 2.

58. Eisenhower had worked with Clay in the Philippines during the interwar period and had trusted him enough to appoint him governor of Germany from 1945 to 1947; see Weingroff, "The President's Man," 2. For Eisenhower's diary about a long and confidential conversation he had with Clay about running for a second term in 1956, see *Eisenhower Diaries*, 288-291.

59. Rose, *Interstate*, 75; Weingroff, *The President's Man*, 4.

60. Rose, *Interstate*, 75.

61. Rose, 75.

62. Rose, 76; Weingroff, "The President's Man," 4-5.

63. Lewis, *Divided Highways*, 111.

64. Lewis, 111.

65. Rose, *Interstate*, 76.

66. Lewis, *Divided Highways*, 111.

67. Lewis, 110-111; Rose, *Interstate*, 75-76; Anthony J. Badger, *Albert Gore, Sr.* (Philadelphia: University of Pennsylvania Press, 2019), 100-101.

68. General Lucius D. Clay, "A New National Highway Program," and "The National Municipal Policy on the New Highway Program" (in the same document), December 1, 1954. I thank Richard Weingroff who provided me with a copy of this document.

69. Clay, "Highway Program," 4.

70. Clay, 1-3.

71. Clay, 4.

72. Clay, "National Municipal Policy," 2.

73. Clay, "Highway Program," 6.

CHAPTER 4. CONGRESS RESURGENT: THE DEFEAT OF THE EISENHOWER HIGHWAY BILL IN 1955

1. See Lewis, *Divided Highways*, 111-112.

2. See chapter 4.

3. E.g., Ambrose, *Eisenhower*, 2:152, 164, 199.

4. Eisenhower anticipated sending the bill on January 27 but was delayed almost a month because members of his administration could not agree on the precise language of the message.

5. *Congressional Record*, Senate, January 18, 1955, 473-474.

6. Ronald L. Heinemann, *Harry Byrd of Virginia* (Richmond: University Press of Virginia, 1996).

7. *Congressional Record*, Senate, May 25, 1955, 6996.

8. Lewis, *Divided Highways*, 114.
9. "Congress Awaits Major Messages," *New York Times*, January 24, 1955.
10. Bragdon Memorandum for Burns, January 20, 1955 (DDEL: Eno Center), 1.
11. William Bragg Ewald, *Eisenhower the President* (Englewood Cliffs, NJ: Prentice-Hall, 1981), 65.
12. Ewald, *Eisenhower*, 89: Clay was someone whom Eisenhower "would have trusted with his life."
13. Bragdon for Burns, January 20, 1955, 1.
14. Bragdon for Burns, January 20, 1955, 2.
15. Byrd would write directly to the Comptroller General's Office on February 17. For the Office's reply, see above.
16. Bragdon for Burns, January 20, 1955, 2.
17. Bragdon Memorandum for Burns, January 24, 1955 (DDEL/Eno Center), 1.
18. Bragdon to Burns, January 24, 1955, 1.
19. Bragdon to Burns, January 24, 1955, 1. Syntactically, it is unclear who the "he" is in the second sentence. The location of "Governor Adams" suggests that it was possibly Adams.
20. Bragdon to Burns, January 27, 1955 (DDEL/Eno), 1.
21. Lewis, *Divided Highways*, 111–112.
22. Bragdon to Burns, January 20, 1955, 2. See above.
23. Bragdon to Burns, February 1, 1955 (DDEL/Eno), 1. Bragdon notes that "the words in parentheses were added."
24. Bragdon to Burns, February 1, 1955, 1.
25. Memorandum of call from Eisenhower to Clay, February 7, 1955 (DDEL/Eno Center). In a separate memorandum from the same day, the subcommittee is described as a "committee to publicize and support the road building program"; see Memorandum, February 7, 1955, in *Eisenhower Papers*, vol. 16, pt. 7, chap. 14, 1556.
26. Bragdon to Burns, February 10, 1955 (DDEL/Eno).
27. Bragdon to Burns, February 10, 1955.
28. Bragdon to Burns, February 8, 1955 (DDEL/Eno), 1.
29. Memorandum from Arthur Minnich to Director Hughes, February 16, 1955 (DDEL: Minnich File), 1.
30. Minnich to Hughes, February 16, 1955, 1.
31. Myron George was actually the second-ranking GOP member of the Roads Subcommittee; the ranking member was sick.
32. James Hagerty, notes of Eisenhower meeting with committee chairs and ranking members, February 21, 1955 (DDEL: Hagerty Diary), 1–2.
33. Hagerty notes, February 21, 1955, 2.
34. Hagerty notes, 2.
35. Hagerty notes, 3.
36. Hagerty notes, 3.
37. Hagerty notes, 2–3.
38. Hagerty notes, 3.

39. Anthony Badger, *Albert Gore, Sr.* (Philadelphia: University of Pennsylvania Press), 89.
40. Badger, *Gore*, 92–99.
41. Badger, 89.
42. *Congressional Record*, House, February 22, 1955, 1904.
43. *Congressional Record*, 1904.
44. *Congressional Record*, 1905.
45. *Congressional Record*, 1905.
46. Richard F. Weingroff, "Kill the Bill: Why the U.S. House of Representatives Rejected the Interstate System in 1955,"19, US Department of Transportation, Federal Highway Administration, Highway History, https://www.fhwa.dot.gov/infrastructure/killbill.cfm.
47. Consider Eric Jaffe, "The Psychological Study of Smiling," *Psychological Science*, February 11, 2011, https://www.psychologicalscience.org/observer/the-psychological-study-of-smiling.
48. "U.S. Highway Plan Assailed by Byrd," *New York Times*, March 19, 1955.
49. "U.S. Highway Plan Assailed by Byrd."
50. "Humphrey Offers Rise in 'Gas' Tax," *New York Times*, March 23, 1955.
51. Rose, *Interstate*, 79 and 146n33.
52. "National Highway Program: Hearing before a Subcommittee of the Committee on Public Works, United States Senate" (Washington, DC: United States Government Printing Office, 1955).
53. "National Highway Program," 610.
54. "National Highway Program," 610.
55. "National Highway Program," 614.
56. "Analysis of the Eisenhower Highway Program," Research Division—Democratic National Committee, April 20, 1955.
57. Dwight D. Eisenhower, "The President's News Conference—March 30, 1955," American Presidency Project, 12, https://www.presidency.ucsb.edu/documents/the-presidents-news-conference-328.
58. Eisenhower, "President's News Conference," 13.
59. *Eisenhower Papers*, vol. 16, pt. 7, chap. 15, 1413.
60. "Senate Unit Votes 5-year Road Plan; Bars a Bond Issue. Ignores President's Request on Financing—Asks Cent Rise in Gasoline Tax," *New York Times*, April 30, 1955.
61. Richard Weingroff, "Kill the Bill," 4.
62. Weingroff, "Kill the Bill," 21.
63. Weingroff, 5.
64. Weingroff, 5.
65. Minnich to Hughes, May 24, 1955, 1–2.
66. Minnich to Hughes, 2.
67. Rose, *Interstate*, 80.
68. Minnich to Hughes, May 24, 1955, 2.
69. Minnich to Hughes, 2.

70. *Congressional Record*, Senate, May 25, 1955, 6967.

71. *Congressional Record*, Senate, May 25, 1955, 7018.

72. Jenner's McCarthyism is well known. For Butler, see "John M. Butler, 80; M'Carthy [sic] Supporter: Ex-Senator Sponsored Legislation to Ban the Communist Party," *New York Times*, March 17, 1978.

73. "Schoeppel Backs Taft," *New York Times*, December 7, 1951.

74. See "Money, Anyone?," *Time*, June 6, 1960, https://web.archive.org/web/20070714044914/http://www.time.com/time/magazine/article/0,9171,874101,00.html.

75. Badger, *Gore*, 105.

76. Weingroff, "Kill the Bill," 2.

77. Weingroff, 6.

78. US Department of Transportation, *American's Highways 1776–1976* (Washington, DC: Government Printing Office, 1976).

79. Confusingly, *America's Highways* claims that Turner influenced the Clay Committee, but it also claims that it was Turner's idea to raise excise taxes on automotive fuel and parts and to create a highway trust fund. Clay's plan did none of this, but instead proposed raising the fuel tax alone in order to replay the government corporation's bonds. It was the Fallon plan that proposed raising user taxes across the broad and that created the highway trust fund. See page 186.

80. Weingroff, "Kill the Bill," 6–7.

81. Weingroff, 8.

82. *Congressional Record—Daily Digest*, July 11, 1955, D493.

83. See David Frum, *How We Got Here* (New York: Basic Books, 2000), 276. Ways and Means lost this power in the 1970s as a consequence of bribery scandals and the reforms that resulted.

84. *Congressional Record—Daily Digest*, July 11, 1955, D493.

85. Weingroff, "Kill the Bill," 9.

86. Weingroff, 9.

87. Dwight Eisenhower, "The President's News Conference—June 29, 1955," American Presidency Project, 13, https://www.presidency.ucsb.edu/documents/the-presidents-news-conference-339.

88. *Congressional Record—Daily Digest*, July 11, 1955, D493.

89. Weingroff, "Kill the Bill," 9–10.

90. Weingroff, 9.

91. Weingroff, 9.

92. "House to Restudy Highway Project," *New York Times*, July 19, 1955; Weingroff, "Kill the Bill," 10.

93. "2 Highway Plans Killed by House," *New York Times*, July 28, 1955.

94. Weingroff, "Kill the Bill," 10.

95. Weingroff, 10. I am indebted to Eric Schickler, Sean Theriault, and Zac McGee for helping me better understand these congressional intricacies.

96. *Congressional Record*, House, July 27, 1955, 11691.

97. Weingroff, "Kill the Bill," 22.

98. Interview of Frank Turner by Dr. John Greenwood, in Weingroff, "Kill the Bill," 17. Weingroff points out that Turner's claim was exaggerated, but that the first fifty votes did still oppose the Fallon bill "by a wide margin."

CHAPTER 5. THE FINAL PUSH AND CONGRESSIONAL VICTORY

1. "2 Highway Plans Billed by House," *New York Times*, July 28, 1955.

2. Weingroff, "Kill the Bill," 16.

3. John D. Morris, "President Rebuffed in Road Plan Plea," *New York Times*, July 29, 1955.

4. Morris, "President Rebuffed."

5. Morris, "President Rebuffed."

6. Dwight D. Eisenhower, "President's Press Conference," August 4, 1955, American Presidency Project, 7–9, https://www.presidency.ucsb.edu/documents/the-presidents-news-conference-336.

7. Eisenhower, "President's Press Conference," 9.

8. Memorandum from George Humphrey to Sherman Adams, August 16, 1955 (DDEL: Official File Box 730, Eisenhower Papers).

9. Adams, *Firsthand Report*, 186.

10. Memorandum from Maxwell Rabb to Sherman Adams, September 26, 1955 (DDEL/Eno Center).

11. "Cabinet Paper—Privileged," September 29, 1955 (DDEL/Eno Center), 1.

12. "Minutes of Cabinet Meeting," September 30, 1955 (DDEL/Eno Center), 4.

13. Memorandum from Max Rabb to President Eisenhower, October 6, 1955 (DDEL/Eno Center), 2 (my italics).

14. "Cabinet Paper—Privileged," October 1, 1955 (DDEL/Eno Center), 2.

15. Rose, *Interstate*, 86.

16. Rose, 86.

17. "Minutes of Cabinet Meeting," October 28, 1955 (DDEL: Ann Whitman File, Eisenhower Papers), 4.

18. Memorandum from Dan T. Smith to George Humphrey, November 4, 1955 (DDEL/Eno Center).

19. Rose, *Interstate*, 87–89.

20. Dwight D. Eisenhower, "Annual Message to the Congress on the State of the Union," January 5, 1956, American Presidency Project, https://www.presidency.ucsb.edu/documents/annual-message-the-congress-the-state-the-union-11.

21. Memorandum from L. A. Minnich to Rowland R. Hughes, January 31, 1956 (DDEL/Eno Center), 1.

22. "Draft: The Interstate Highway System Fund," February 8, 1956 (DDEL/Eno Center), 2.

23. "Draft," February 8, 1956, 1.

24. "House Democrats Set on Road Plan," *New York Times*, February 7, 1956.

Cooper's first name was Jere, not Joel; see Tara Mitchell Mielnik, "Jere Cooper," *Tennessee Encyclopedia*, https://tennesseeencyclopedia.net/entries/jere-cooper/.

25. Weingroff, "Kill the Bill," 23.

26. "Highway Revenue Act of 1956: Hearings before the Committee on Ways and Means, House of Representatives" (Washington, DC: United States Government Printing Office, 1956), 24.

27. "Hearings before the Committee on Ways and Means," 24.

28. "Hearings before the Committee on Ways and Means," 25.

29. "Hearings before the Committee on Ways and Means," 41.

30. Weingroff, "Kill the Bill," 23.

31. Rose, *Interstate*, 89.

32. Dwight Eisenhower, "The President's News Conference," April 25, 1956, American Presidency Project, https://www.presidency.ucsb.edu/documents/the-presidents-news-conference-300.

33. Rose, *Interstate*, 89.

34. Rose, 92.

CONCLUSION

1. Neustadt, *Presidential Leadership*.

2. Greenstein, *Hidden-Hand Presidency*.

3. Erwin Hargrove, *The President as Leader* (Lawrence: University Press of Kansas, 1998).

4. See "All the President's Doodles," *The Atlantic*, September 2006, https://www.theatlantic.com/magazine/archive/2006/09/all-the-presidents-doodles/305115/.

5. As Nichols has shown, the extent to which the so-called modern presidency is either an innovation on or departure from the presidency as envisioned by the Constitution itself has been exaggerated by scholars. See David Nichols, *The Myth of the Modern Presidency* (University Park: Pennsylvania State University Press, 1994).

6. See Andrew Rudalevige, *Managing the President's Agenda* (Princeton, NJ: Princeton University Press, 2002).

7. My claim is not that Eisenhower pursued such a presidency-centered legislative strategy in all cases, only that his decision to sideline Congress regarding the marquee domestic legislative program of his first presidential term signals conformity with the model of the modern presidency, which Eisenhower is frequently described as eschewing.

8. Eisenhower, *Eisenhower Diaries*, 231.

9. Eisenhower, 231.

10. E.g., John Dearborn, *Power Shifts* (Chicago: University of Chicago Press, 2021); Tulis, *Rhetorical Presidency*; Daniel Stid, *The President as Statesman* (Lawrence: University Press of Kansas, 1998).

11. Sidney Milkis, *The President and the Parties* (New York: Oxford University Press, 1993).

12. See Nichols, *Myth of the Modern Presidency*; Stephen J. Wayne, *The Legislative Presidency* (New York: Harper and Row, 1978).

13. Tulis, *Rhetorical Presidency*.

14. Patrick O'Brien, *Presidential Control over Administration* (Lawrence: University Press of Kansas, 2022); Dearborn, *Power Shifts*; John Burke, *The Institutional Presidency*, 2nd ed. (Baltimore: Johns Hopkins University Press, 2000).

15. E.g., William Howell and Terry Moe, *Presidents, Populists, and the Crisis of Democracy* (Chicago: University of Chicago Press, 2020).

16. E.g., Anthony James Joes, "Eisenhower Revisionism: The Tide Comes In," *Presidential Studies Quarterly* 15, no. 3 (1985): 561–71; Ambrose, *Eisenhower*, 2:250.

BIBLIOGRAPHIC ESSAY

To my knowledge, there is no single book dedicated to discussing Dwight Eisenhower's role in passing the 1956 Federal Highway Act. The two most comprehensive, in-depth accounts of that subject have been written from the perspective of transportation history in the United States—Mark Rose, *Interstate: Express Highway Politics 1939–1989* (Knoxville: University of Tennessee Press, 1990), and Tom Lewis, *Divided Highways* (Ithaca, NY: Cornell University Press, 2013). Additionally, some of the most valuable writings on Eisenhower's relationship with federal highway policy have not been published as books or in academic journals. Richard Weingroff, historian at the Federal Highway Administration (FHA), and Jeff Davis, senior fellow at the Eno Center for Transportation, have authored numerous, painstakingly detailed essays on this topic. Their writings can be found, respectively, on the FHA website (Highway History: https://www.fhwa.dot.gov/infrastructure/public roads.cfm) and the Eno Center website (https://www.enotrans.org/).

There are numerous writings on the history of US roadbuilding before and leading up to the 1956 Act, but three stand out for different reasons: FHA, *America's Highways, 1776–1976* (Washington, DC: US Government Printing Office, 1976), is useful as a chronological repository of information about roadbuilding from the American colonial era up to the creation of the federal highway system; Stephen Minicucci, "Internal Improvements and the Union, 1790–1860," *Studies in American Political Development* 18 (Fall 2004), 160–185, elaborates a compelling argument about the fitful development of US infrastructure during the nineteenth century; and Katherine Johnson, *The American Road* (Lawrence: University Press of Kansas, 2021), examines US highway history from the standpoint of American political development.

Several biographies and biographical writings that discuss Eisenhower also mention his role in passing federal highway expansion, but none of these offer an in-depth treatment of that role. The two most prominent Eisenhower biographies are Stephen Ambrose, *Eisenhower*, vol. 2, *The President* (New York: Simon and Schuster, 1984), and Jean Edward Smith, *Eisenhower in War and Peace* (New York: Random House,

2013). For biographical writings that attempt to derive leadership principles from Eisenhower's major policy decisions, see Susan Eisenhower, *How Ike Led: The Principles behind Eisenhower's Biggest Decisions* (New York: Thomas Dunne Books, 2020), and Peter Norton, "Be Like Ike," *The Miller Center Series on Issues & Policy*, January 10, 2017: https://millercenter.org/issues-policy/economics/be-like-ike. The edited volume *Reexamining the Eisenhower Presidency*, ed. Shirley Warshaw (New York: Praeger, 1993), includes essays examining various aspects of the Eisenhower administration, though none touch directly on the highway program.

Political scientists and presidency scholars have authored a number of writings that, although not taking up Eisenhower and federal highways directly or explicitly, can nevertheless help those interested in that subject make better sense of it. Perhaps the best political science book on Eisenhower is Fred Greenstein, *The Hidden-Hand Presidency*, 2nd ed. (Baltimore: Johns Hopkins University Press, 1994). However, Greenstein does not discuss the Federal Highway Act directly, instead focusing on other policy areas that preoccupied Eisenhower. Similarly, the classic Richard Neustadt, *Presidential Power and the Modern Presidents* (New York: The Free Press, 1990), contains a fine discussion of Eisenhower's leadership style, but again, no direct treatment of federal highway expansion. Other relevant writings include William Howell, *Power without Persuasion* (Princeton, NJ: Princeton University Press, 2003); Andrew Rudalevige, *Managing the President's Program* (Princeton, NJ: Princeton University Press, 2002), and Rudalevige, *By Executive Order* (Princeton, NJ: Princeton University Press, 2021); Richard P. Nathan, *The Administrative Presidency* (New York: Wiley, 1983); Jeffrey K. Tulis, *The Rhetorical Presidency* (Princeton, NJ: Princeton University Press, 2017); Daniel Stid, *The President as Statesman* (Lawrence: University Press of Kansas, 1998); Stephen Skowronek, *The Politics Presidents Make* (Cambridge, MA: The Belknap Press of Harvard University Press, 1997); Erwin Hargrove, *The President as Leader* (Lawrence: University Press of Kansas, 1998); John Burke, *The Institutional Presidency*, 2nd ed. (Baltimore: Johns Hopkins University Press, 2000); and Patrick O'Brien, *Presidential Control over Administration* (Lawrence: University Press of Kansas, 2022). For a helpful overview of contending scholarly assessments of Eisenhower since the appearance of Greenfield, *Hidden-Hand*

Presidency, see Anthony James Joes, "Eisenhower Revisionism: The Tide Comes In," *Presidential Studies Quarterly* 15, no. 3 (1985): 561–71.

The Dwight D. Eisenhower Presidential Library in Abilene, Kansas, is a treasure trove of information relevant to the Federal Highway Act, but for those unable to get there, there are several writings and collections that provide up-close information about the Eisenhower presidency. Eisenhower's first chief of staff, Sherman Adams, wrote a lengthy and detailed account of his time in the Eisenhower White House: Adams, *Firsthand Report* (New York: Harper & Brothers, 1961). Additional writings authored by individuals who were personally familiar with Eisenhower are William Bragg Ewald, *Eisenhower the President* (Englewood Cliffs, NJ: Prentice-Hall, 1981), and Stephen Hess, "What Congress Looked Like from Inside the Eisenhower White House," Brookings, January 6, 2012: https://www.brookings.edu/research/what-congress-looked-like-from-inside-the-eisenhower-white-house/. Eisenhower himself authored two books during his retirement from the presidency, each of which contains interesting anecdotes about federal highways: Dwight D. Eisenhower, *Mandate for Change* (New York: Doubleday, 1963), and Eisenhower, *At Ease: Stories I Tell to Friends* (New York: Eastern Acorn Press, 1981). Edited selections from Eisenhower's personal diaries have been published as a standalone book: Eisenhower, *The Eisenhower Diaries*, ed. Robert Ferrell (New York: Norton, 1981). Outside of the Eisenhower Library archives, the best resource for obtaining Eisenhower's personal documents and writings is Eisenhower, *The Papers of Dwight David Eisenhower*, 21 vols., ed. Louis Galambos (Baltimore: Johns Hopkins University Press, 1971).

INDEX

Adams, Sherman
  on 1954 midterms, 54
  Bragdon's standoff with, 49–50
  Eisenhower's biography, 147
  highway legislation plan of, 29, 30, 33–35, 38, 43–46, 48, 57, 71, 96
  Humphrey's memorandum to, 111
  organization of presidential committees, 43–47, 54, 55, 58, 63, 70, 135n15
  as presidential advisor, 112, 135n18
  Rabb's memorandum to, 112
  on Republican leaders, 136n40
Allen, George E., 18
Ambrose, Stephen, 4, 5, 18, 134n1, 145
American Association of State Highway Officials, 14
American Municipal Association (AMA), 60, 61, 62, 66
American Transportation Association, 102
American Trucking Association, 60
Atomic Energy Commission, 83
Augusta National Golf Course, 18
Autobahn (German national highway system), 3–4, 129n6
automobile industry, 14–15

Bacon, Donald C., 53
Bane, Frank, 47
Barnard, Chester, 47
Bechtel, Stephen, 47, 50
Beck, Dave, 50, 51, 108, 109
Benson, Ezra Taft, 112
Beschloss, Michael, 18
bicycles, 12–13
Boggs, Hale, 6, 101, 118–119, 121, 125
Boggs-Fallon bill, 118–119, 121–122
Bragdon, John Stewart
  on Clay plan, 69–70, 75, 77
  discussion of highway legislation, 29, 30–31, 34–35, 38, 43, 44, 49, 57–58, 63, 72, 73, 113
  on funding mechanism of highway bill, 71, 74, 76, 78
  on Moses-Tallamy plan, 48–49

"National Defense Highway Bill"
  draft, 32–33, 35
  on organization of the highway authority, 78–79
  standoff with Adams, 49–50
Bricker Amendment, 17
Bridges, Styles, 80
Buckley, Charles, 81
Buckner, Helen Watson, 132n5
Buckner, Walker G., 22, 23, 24
  background of, 132n5
  donations to Republican Party, 132n5
  Eisenhower and, 25, 44
  highway expansion plan, 29, 30, 31, 32–33, 35, 37, 38, 51, 104, 105
Bureau of Public Roads (BPR)
  creation of, 21, 33
  funds for public works, 29
  leadership of, 14, 24–25, 29
  responsibilities of, 15, 49
Burns, Arthur, 26, 28–29, 30, 31, 35, 48, 49, 69–70
Bush, Prescott, 94–95
Butler, John, 97
Byrd, Harry Flood, Sr.
  career of, 106
  on corporate bonds, 96
  criticism of the Clay bill, 67–68, 69, 71–72, 82, 86, 88–89, 90, 91, 92, 93, 117
  legislative priorities, 66–67
  work in Senate Finance Committee, 68, 78
Byrnes, John, 119

Campbell, Joseph, 7, 90, 91–92, 93
Case, Francis, 81
Chavez, Dennis, 81, 97, 125
China, 54–55
Civilian Conservation Corps (CCC), 13–14
Clay, Henry, 58
Clay, Lucius D.
  as advisor to Eisenhower, 7, 52, 58, 113
  career of, 137n58

Clay, Lucius D., *continued*
  as chair of the PAC, 50–51, 56, 58, 59, 64, 123, 135n15
  personality of, 39, 58–59, 64, 65
  taxation policy, 60–61
Clay Committee, 10, 57, 67, 140n79
Clay highway bill
  congressional debates on, 80, 94, 106
  contradictions of, 92
  criticism of, 67–68, 69, 74, 86–87, 93
  Democrats' view of, 82–83, 93, 103–104
  distribution of, 70
  drafting of, 19, 38, 90
  feedback from the state governors, 63–64, 115
  financing mechanism, 61–62, 67, 68, 74–78, 81, 83, 86–89, 91–93, 96, 111
  presentation to the Congress, 66, 85–86
  presidential support of, 84–85, 88, 106, 125
  press coverage of, 69, 89
  Senate rejection of, 5, 94, 95, 99, 108
  White House meetings on, 70, 72–74, 80–82
Collyer, John, 48
Colt, Sloan, 50, 51, 52
Cooper, Jere, 118, 120
Council of Economic Advisors (CEA), 26

Davis, Jeff, 145
Democratic Party
  1954 midterm elections, 6–7, 37, 65
  Eisenhower and, 37, 38, 46, 66
  foreign policy, 66
  highway expansion plan, 1, 5, 6, 46, 81, 118
Dewey, Thomas, 23, 53
Dodge, Joseph, 25, 26, 29, 35
Dondero, George, 1–2, 44, 45, 81, 95, 98, 99, 103
du Pont, Francis Victor
  Adams's recommendation of, 44
  criticism of Clay bill, 72, 74
  Eisenhower and, 45
  as head of the Bureau of Public Roads, 24, 25, 29, 70

highway expansion plan, 31–32, 33, 38, 48, 49, 57–58, 73, 76, 79, 134n8
Durkin, Martin, 131n35
Dwight D. Eisenhower Presidential Library, 147

Eisenhower, Dwight D.
  1954 midterms and, 9–10, 53, 54, 56
  advisors of, 7, 20, 50–52, 58, 135n18
  appointments, 125
  background and education, 15, 19
  biographies of, 4, 5, 145–106, 147
  on Boggs-Fallon bill, 121
  business elites and, 18–20, 65, 125, 127–108, 131n31
  cabinet meetings, 112
  civilian career, 16
  Clay's relationship with, 70, 137n58
  commitment to free trade, 16–17
  congressional policy, 36–38, 52, 53–54, 65–66, 105–106
  Democrats and, 46, 65, 84, 88
  design of presidential office of, 125–126
  du Pont family and, 134n8
  Fallon bill and, 101–102, 108, 109
  favorite news source of, 20
  fiscal policy, 17, 24, 33, 117
  foreign policy, 54–55
  Gore bill and, 87, 95, 108
  on government corporation, 94
  Governors' Conference speech, 39, 40, 41–42, 48, 64
  Hearst statement, 21–22, 25
  Hollywood Bowl speech, 53–54, 55
  illness of, 1, 112, 113, 116–117, 122
  leadership style, 94, 124, 126
  legislative strategy, 7, 8–9, 55, 64–65, 88, 100, 106, 107, 110–111, 126, 128, 142n7
  Lyndon Johnson and, 54
  memo to Dodge, 25, 26
  memo to Hauge, 23–24
  military service of, 15–16
  on New Deal governance, 21–22
  Nixon and, 39, 134n1
  on nomination of comptroller general, 93
  personality of, 63, 72–73, 124, 125, 126

INDEX 151

political philosophy of, 16, 17
presentation of highway legislation, 80, 85–86
presidential campaign, 15, 16, 17–18
presidential decisions, 6, 10, 81, 123
public works program of, 25–27
Republicans and, 37–38, 54
State of the Union address, 16, 21, 26, 85, 116
support of Clay plan, 80–82, 84–85, 87, 89, 111
view of separation of powers, 7–8, 9, 17, 130n17
weekly legislative conference, 79
writings of, 147
Eisenhower's highway program
background of, 2–4, 129n6
cost of, 39, 40
deadlock, 35–38
defeat of, 90, 105
development of, 7, 8, 10, 17
funding mechanism, 4–6, 30, 41
legislative strategy for, 8, 10, 75, 127–128
presentation to the Congress, 38, 39, 40–41, 80, 85–86
proposed budget, 40–41, 42
Senate debate on, 5, 7, 96–97
stalemate of, 44–45
study groups, 7
timeline, 45–46, 75, 78
White House meetings on, 75–77

Fallon, George, 81, 99, 100–101, 105, 106, 125, 140n79
Fallon bill
defeat of, 105, 108, 109
Democrats and, 109
Eisenhower's position on, 101–102, 108, 109
funding of, 6, 107
highway users and, 102, 108–109, 121
House debate on, 99, 102–104, 108
preparation of, 98, 100, 107
Public Works Committee approval of, 103, 121
revenue component of, 103
tax component of, 5, 100–101, 102

Federal-Aid Highway Act (1916), 13
Federal-Aid Highway Act (1954), 86
Federal-Aid Highway Act (1956)
drafts of, 32–33, 35
financing mechanisms, 15, 33
legislative process and, 1, 2–3, 10, 122
scholarship on, 4, 145
supporters of, 38
Federal Highway Administration (FHA), 145
Federal Highway Corporation, 91
Fillmore, Millard, 126
Folsom, Marion, 71
Formosa standoff, 54–55

"the gang," 18, 131n31
gasoline tax increase, 97–98, 100–102
George, Myron, 81
Good Roads Movement, 5, 13
Gore, Albert, Sr., 81, 83, 87, 96, 125
as chair of Subcommittee on Public Roads, 88, 89, 90, 92
Gore bill (Senate Bill 1048)
funding of, 83–84, 97, 98
House debates on, 98
introduction of, 5–6, 83, 88, 106–107
Senate discussion of, 95, 97
states benefited from, 97
subcommittee vote on, 94
governors' committee on highways, 115–116
Governors' Conference, 39, 40, 41–42, 43
Great Society programs, 6
Greenstein, Fred, 7, 63
The Hidden-Hand Presidency, 124

Hagerty, James, 27, 51, 54, 81, 82, 83
Halleck, Charles, 80
Hardeman, D. B., 53
Harrison, William Henry, 126
Hauge, Gabriel
Eisenhower's assignment to, 24, 25
formation of the PAC and, 47, 51, 54, 135n25
highway expansion plans and, 29, 30, 31, 38, 50
Heinemann, Ronald, 67
Helms, Paul Hoy, 1, 94

152 INDEX

Hess, Stephen, 7, 8
highway expansion
    Adams's plan, 45–64, 55, 58, 63, 65, 70
    background and context of, 11–20
    Buckner's plan, 22–23, 24, 29
    Eisenhower's role in, 2–6, 8, 11, 17, 21, 26, 27–29, 30–31, 42
    government committees on, 28–35
    governors' committee view of, 115–116
    maintenance budget, 15
    Moses-Tallamy plan for, 33–34, 35, 37, 41, 48, 57
    pre-modern era, 11–15
    presidential support of, 129n12
    purpose of, 28
    special session of Congress on, 110
    uncertainty about, 35, 59–60
Highway Trust Fund, 4–5, 117–118, 119, 120–101, 140n79
Hoover, Herbert Clark, 53
House Public Works Committee, 98, 100, 102–103
House Rules Committee, 103
House Ways and Means Committee
    authority of, 101, 107
    Boggs-Fallon bill, 121
    bribery scandals, 140n84
    Fallon bill and, 101, 102, 103, 108
    gasoline tax increase, 97–98
    hearings of, 121
    Humphrey's testimony before, 119
    reform of, 140n84
    responsibilities of, 100
Hughes, Rowland R., 72, 79, 95, 96
Humphrey, George
    attitude to Clay plan, 89–90, 115, 120
    Bragdon's meeting with, 72
    Eisenhower's relationship with, 45, 70
    Fallon bill and, 102
    highway program of, 38, 46, 76, 96, 112–113, 115, 119, 120–121
    idea of Highway Trust Fund, 117–118, 119, 120
    legislative strategy of, 36, 111
    memorandum to Adams, 111, 112, 114
    on organization of the highway authority, 78
    on public works program, 27
    testimony before Gore's committee, 89, 91
    testimony before the Ways and Means Committee, 119, 120–121

Inter-Agency Committee (IAC)
    highway legislation, 53, 56–57
    leadership of, 44, 46–47, 48, 113
    members of, 43, 45, 70
    relationships with the PAC, 58, 59, 69, 70–71, 92

Jenner, William, 97
Johnson, Lyndon B. (LBJ), 6, 8, 54, 83
Johnson, Robert, 47, 54
Jones, W. Alton, 18

Karsten, Frank, 120
Kennedy, John F., 19
Knowland, William, 80, 95, 96–97
Kohler, Walter J., Jr., 50, 112
Korean War, 27–28, 35
Kyes, Roger, 44, 46–47, 48, 51, 64, 65, 135n19

Lausche, Frank, 116
legislative authority, 127
Lewis, Tom, 29, 58, 59, 74
Long, Robert, 92
Lovett, Robert A., 39

MacArthur, Douglas, 15
MacDonald, Thomas Harris, 13–14, 24–25, 31, 33
Marshall, George, 15, 16
Martin, Edward, 81, 91, 92, 95, 96, 97
Martin, Jack, 70–71, 73, 112
Martin, Joseph, 44, 46, 108, 110
McCormick, Robert, 20
Minnich, Arthur, 50, 80, 95, 117
modern presidency, 142n5
Morris, John D., 109
Moses, Robert, 33–34, 48, 57, 70
Moses-Tallamy plan for highway expansion, 33–34, 35, 37, 41, 48, 57
Murray, Robert, 29–30, 31, 32, 133n26
Muskie, Ed, 97

INDEX   153

Neustadt, Richard, 124
New Deal programs
  Eisenhower's attitude toward, 16, 17, 19, 22, 24
  highway expansion and, 14
New Presidential Advisory Committee. *See* Weeks Committee
Nichols, David, 142n5
1954 midterm election, 6–7, 9–10, 36, 37, 53–56, 65
Nixon, Richard, 39, 42, 47, 55, 64, 134n1
North Atlantic Treaty Organization (NATO), 16

Office of Public Roads, 13–14

Palmer, James, 47
Patman, John William Wright, 103, 104
Payne, Frederick, 97
presidential decisions, 2–3, 6, 123, 127
President's Advisory Committee (PAC)
  authority of, 52
  composition of, 51
  conflict of interest in, 51, 52
  creation of, 51, 63, 134n15
  dissolution of, 98
  failure of, 123
  goals of, 43, 51–52
  highway legislation of, 53, 56, 57, 60–61
  leadership of, 46–47, 48, 50–51, 123, 135n15
  lobbying groups and, 60
  members of, 43–44, 51, 55–56
  public relations, 77–78
  relationships with the IAC, 58, 59, 70–71, 92
  responsibilities of, 45–46
  taxation and, 60–61
Progressive Republicanism, 17
public works programs, 26–27

Quemoy island crisis (Formosa standoff), 54–55

Rabb, Maxwell, 112, 113
Rayburn, Sam, 53–54, 100, 103, 105, 108, 109

Reagan, Ronald, 134n9
Republican Party
  1954 midterm elections, 6–7, 53, 56
  donations to, 132n5
  Eisenhower's relations with, 37–38, 54, 66
  reform of, 53
Reynolds & Co., 22
roadbuilding, 12–14, 15, 26, 145. *See also* highway expansion
Roberts, Clifford, 18
Roberts, William A., 50
Robinson, William, 18
Roosevelt, Franklin Delano, 8, 16, 53, 124
Roosevelt, Theodore, 134n9
Rose, Mark, 27–28, 32, 56, 57, 95, 100, 121
Rudalevige, Andrew, 126

Schoeppel, Andrew, 97
Schwartz, Gary, 134n8
Sentner, David, 110
separation of powers, 7–8, 53, 126
Simpson, Richard M., 101
Slater, Ellis D., 18
Smith, Dan Throop, 115
Smith, Jean Edward, 5
  Eisenhower in War and Peace, 145
Smith, Merriam, 93, 94
Social Security Fund, 118
Stephens, Thomas E., 50
Stevenson, Adlai, 16
Symington, Stuart, 91

Taft, Robert A., 37, 97
Tallamy, Bertram D., 33–34, 48, 57, 70
Tennessee Valley Authority, 83
Thompson, Glen, 42
toll roads, 116
truckers, 60, 108–109, 114, 121
Truman, Harry S., 8, 124
Turner, Frank, 72, 74, 98, 104, 134n8, 140n79

unemployment, 28
United Nations, 16, 17
United States
  comptroller general, 90
  Constitution, 127

United States, *continued*
   Federal Highway System, 4
   political authority in, 12
   post-war economy, 3–4
US Commerce Department, 29–30
US Congress
   1954 midterm elections, 6–7, 36
   legislative role of, 8–9
US House of Representatives
   debates on highway bill, 2, 99–100, 105
   See also specific House committees
US Senate
   committees, 83, 88
   debates and vote on highway bill, 1, 2, 5, 105

Warren, Lindsay Carter, 90
Watson, Thomas J., 132n5
Weeks, Sinclair, 24, 29, 45, 72, 79, 112, 114–116
Weeks Committee
   formation of, 112, 113
   highway plan of, 114–115, 116
   report to cabinet, 114
   responsibilities, 113–114
   truckers' meeting with, 114
Weingroff, Richard, 134n15, 145
White, Theodore H., 105
Williams, John, 97
Willis, Charles F., Jr., 47, 48, 64, 135n25
Wilson, Charles, 19, 44, 112
Wilson, Woodrow, 13, 14, 15, 24, 53

ABOUT THE AUTHOR

Charles U. Zug is assistant professor of political science and Kinder Institute Assistant Professor of Constitutional Democracy at the University of Missouri. He is the author of *Demagogues in American Politics* (Oxford University Press, 2022) and numerous journal articles.

www.ingramcontent.com/pod-product-compliance
Lightning Source LLC
Chambersburg PA
CBHW030656230426
43665CB00011B/1118